W9-CBU-367

Violent Manhood

J. E. Sumerau

ROWMAN & LITTLEFIELD
Lanham • Boulder • New York • London

Published by Rowman & Littlefield
An imprint of The Rowman & Littlefield Publishing Group, Inc.
4501 Forbes Boulevard, Suite 200, Lanham, Maryland 20706
https://rowman.com

6 Tinworth Street, London SE11 5AL, United Kingdom

Copyright © 2020 by The Rowman & Littlefield Publishing Group, Inc.

All rights reserved. No part of this book may be reproduced in any form or by any electronic or mechanical means, including information storage and retrieval systems, without written permission from the publisher, except by a reviewer who may quote passages in a review.

British Library Cataloguing in Publication Information Available

Library of Congress Cataloging-in-Publication Data

Names: Sumerau, J. E., author.
Title: Violent manhood / J. E. Sumerau.
Description: Lanham : Rowman & Littlefield, 2020. | Includes bibliographical references and index. | Summary: "This book critically examines the way men construct and explain relationships between violence, manhood, and inequality in society"— Provided by publisher.
Identifiers: LCCN 2020012610 (print) | LCCN 2020012611 (ebook) | ISBN 9781538136485 (cloth) | ISBN 9781538136492 (paperback) | ISBN 9781538136508 (epub)
Subjects: LCSH: Men—Identity. | Masculinity—Social aspects. | Violence in men.
Classification: LCC HQ1090 .S876 2020 (print) | LCC HQ1090 (ebook) | DDC 305.31—dc23
LC record available at https://lccn.loc.gov/2020012610
LC ebook record available at https://lccn.loc.gov/2020012611

♾ ™ The paper used in this publication meets the minimum requirements of American National Standard for Information Sciences Permanence of Paper for Printed Library Materials, ANSI/NISO Z39.48-1992.

Contents

Chapter One

Encountering Manhood

Although I do not recall ever wanting to be a man, scars on my mind and body daily remind me how many times other people have sought to convince me I was supposed to become one.[1] When I hear certain sexual and gender slurs on television or elsewhere, for example, my mind races back to the moments such words foretold or times such words arose in the midst of conflict and violence of too many varieties to count. Likewise, when the weather is chillier, I can feel the aches in my legs, shoulders, and back where some markers of past violence can be seen while others have faded, at least in a visible sense. Similarly, when I look in the mirror even years after multiple surgeries, I sometimes still see the facial injuries that once made it hard for me to look at any mirror for more than a few moments. I may not have ever wanted to be a man, but that never seemed to matter to the people trying to convince me otherwise.

At the same time, my experiences navigating this world as a non-binary trans woman misdiagnosed as male at birth served as an advanced class in gender. I think about the times when my body and mannerisms allow me to be seen by others[2] as a potential man. In such cases, people are more likely to listen to what I say, ask for my opinions, defer to me in terms of bodily spacing and verbal articulation, and laugh at my jokes, no matter how poorly I execute them. When I am seen by others as a potential man, however, people are also more likely to react in anger when I show affection for others who may be interpreted as men, when I show any emotion at all, when my voice leaves my mouth in a higher octave, or when I flip my wrist while discussing an especially beautiful song or landscape. These moments repeatedly remind me of the expectations and norms for what it means to be a man in the eyes of other people.

Of course, there are other times when people recognize me as the woman I am, and in so doing, continuously remind me just how differently most people react to women and men in the United States. I think about the ways I suddenly receive less respect for my personal space and have fewer opportunities to be heard. I think about how quickly my opinions become a matter of emotion or something to be discarded, argued against without pause, or merely an overreaction to a given situation. I think of how much more often people will comment on my clothing choices, my body and what they might want to do with parts of it I may or may not possess at the time, and my flowing hair, though I almost never request or invite such commentary. I also think about how I am suddenly expected to have many emotions concerning any particular topic, and how at the same time, such emotions are seen as evidence that my own body and mind might not be worthy of respect or consideration. Put simply, these moments remind me of the pervasive sexism embedded within U.S. social relations, and bring such patterns to life as I mentally compare my treatment as a woman to the ways people treat me when I am seen as a potential man.

In fact, these observations become even more clear in the many cases and situations where I appear to others somewhere between a woman and a man. In such moments, the combination of a beard on my face and a skirt flowing around my knees may lead someone to exclaim—in fear, confusion, or both—and wonder aloud what I am. At other times, the combination of my feminine body language and my broad shoulders may lead someone to slam me into a bathroom wall and/or call me an abomination. There are still other times, in rural and urban areas alike, where a small child who appears to be dressed as a boy may comment kindly on my skirt only to then hear their parent or guardian insult me (usually someone who appears to be a potential man) or tell me I should be ashamed of myself (usually someone who appears to be a potential woman). In these situations, my inability to be easily categorized or read as appropriately performing either manhood or womanhood facilitates panic, anger, and potential violence from others who require binary gender categorization to make sense of the world.

At the heart of each of these examples lies the interactional processes whereby people socially construct the gender of themselves and others based on aspects of appearance, behavior, and/or other socially recognizable cues.[3] Since gender itself has no natural properties,[4] people spend much of their daily lives—consciously or otherwise—searching for clues that will allow them to determine the gender of others and perform their gender identities. Likewise, since people rarely see other people naked in social life, such efforts rely heavily on not only determining the gender of another person but also on assuming that determination of another's gender also tells us something about the composition of said other's body. It is within the context of such interpretive work that what we call *gender* is both established and assumed throughout the entirety of our interactions with ourselves and others.

In this book, I interrogate the social construction of one aspect of the gender spectrum in contemporary U.S. society: manhood. Specifically, I outline the ways that contemporary notions of U.S. manhood are often predicated on and deeply tied to the performance, or at least threat, of violence. Utilizing interviews with cisgender, heterosexual, middle- or upper-class white men concerning prominent gendered and sexual debates in society today, I tease out the ways violence finds voice in contemporary U.S. notions of *what it means to be a man* as well as pathways for social change revealed by the possibility of disaggregating violence and manhood in the minds and actions of people who identify as men. To this end, I draw on a lifetime of experiences like the ones noted above, as well as my own and others' scholarly work concerning the social construction of men and masculinities over time.[5]

The central goal of this book is to identify how people who are assigned male are taught to be violent as part of learning how to claim their identities as men. Further, I outline the ways that these lessons about violence as an essential element of manhood emerge in men's reactions to violence against women; people of color regardless of gender identities; lesbian, gay, bisexual, and transgender (LGBT) people; and one another. I also outline men's opposition to efforts to lessen violence in society. Finally, I illustrate some ways that transforming societal notions of what it means to be a man may be essential to the success of any program, policy, or reform targeted at reducing violence in the United States. In developing these ideas, I encourage readers to shift from viewing violence as "just something men do" to something people *who wish to be seen as men* embrace to be recognized by others as men. As such, I argue that challenging violence ultimately relies on not only changing the things men do, but also revising what it means to be a man in contemporary U.S. society.

HOW A PERSON BECOMES A MAN

One of the hallmarks of gender scholarship over the past half-century is the recognition that men are not born—they are made.[6] Although this may sound strange to anyone socialized by contemporary American notions of inherent or essential manhood, the vast body of research on gender continuously reveals that what it means to be a man—or any other gender identity—arises from a complex set of individual, organizational, and structural patterns that depend on what people do, think, and affirm within and between groups.[7] Especially for readers who are less familiar with these empirical observations, it may be helpful to start our discussion with the processes whereby people begin to become men.

To become a man, first one must be born into a social context where something referred to and known as a "man" already exists.[8] Put simply, one cannot become a man unless there is an identity category already in existence that others will recognize and accept as a man. As identity construction scholars have long noted,[9] the development of any type of self requires some social understanding of the possibility of such a self. Those seeking to be thin, or beautiful, or a soccer player, for example, must first learn what any of these things are from other people before they are able to become them. At the same time, there must be something these things are not (fat or average, ugly or plain, or someone who doesn't play soccer) to distinguish between what one is (soccer player) and what one is not (not a soccer player). Since social life builds on the identities and meanings of previous generations, someone can only become a given gender identity (man, woman, gender-queer, agender, etc.) if there first exists recognition (within a specific group or more broadly) that the given gender identity exists and that there are ways to demonstrate that one is that given gender identity and not a different one.

An illustration of this process of "becoming" any type of social identity or member of a category may be useful here. If, for example, a person is born into a social context (a family, a city, a town, a culture, or other location) in which there is nothing people already know about called a Dreadnought, then that person has no way to become a Dreadnought. If, on the other hand, a person is born into a social context in which the members of that group (family members) or residents of that location (people who live in that city) are devoted fans of a messiah-type, supernatural being called Dreadnought, then said person could be encouraged by others to act like Dreadnought and someday develop into a Dreadnought-type being or character. In fact, it would not be surprising if some readers right now are asking, for example, "What is a Dreadnought?" or "Is a Dreadnought a real thing?" while other readers recognize this reference right away and might wish to be like this character type in their own lives and behaviors.[10] In either case, as social psychologists have long noted, a person can only become a given type of "thing" or "person" or "object" (i.e., develop an identity as a man or a Dreadnought) if there is already a version of that thing, person, or object that others recognize and thus may encourage said person to emulate and, over time, become.

Emerging studies of relationships between religious and non-religious children, families, and communities provide another example of this type of process at work.[11] If, for instance, people are raised in households where family members believe in a higher power they call a god, then these people are likely to understand at some point that there is a god in their home, there are ways to act godly or god-like in their own lives, and there are people who expect them to act in such godly or god-like ways. At the same time, however, when people are raised in households where family members do not believe in or even mention a higher power of any type, they may not understand that there is a god in other people's homes or that they could or should act in a way suggested by such god. For people to know about a god and thus become godly, there must first be a type of god created, promoted, and evidenced in their own social world.

In the contemporary United States, this first step in becoming a man is rarely noted in conversations or discussions about the topic of manhood.[12] This is because assertions of the existence of an identity named man and the ways people should behave to be seen by themselves and others as manly or man-like are constant, widespread, and normal.[13] Whether one looks to religion, science, media, politics, or other cultural meaning systems, said viewer will find narratives or scripts for what a man is, how a man should behave, and how others should behave around such manly or man-like beings. Although the type of manhood promoted by a given source of authority or influence may vary dramatically, both newly born human beings and those who are ushering such beings into our world will consistently be taught that there is something called a man and specific ways a given person may become one.[14]

Within this context, most American media, religion, science, and other powerful systems of meaning align manhood with being assigned male by society at birth.[15] Although many people live as, are seen by themselves and others as, and identify as men without ever having been assigned male at any time or by any social authority, contemporary U.S. society typically defines manhood in relation to male sex assignment and often claims that one who is assigned male by society will and must become a man within the society. As Candace West and Don Zimmerman[16] note, this assigned-sex to performed-gender pathway is a quintessential element in the social construction of the identity *man*, the articulation that such an identity exists, and that this man identity contains specific behaviors, beliefs, practices, and expectations in a given society.

As such, the second step in becoming a man involves being assigned male by social authorities, usually at birth and by medical doctors. When people are assigned male by social authorities, such authorities alongside parents and other significant relations will generally expect them to become men, will identify them as boys who will become men in their own interactions and mental expectations, and will work to create manly or man-like qualities and behaviors that the person in question must perform to avoid punishment, criticism, or other negative results. As Barrie Thorne[17] observed almost 30 years ago, much of childhood thus involves social authorities training people who have been assigned male to learn how to think, behave, and react in ways culturally expected of those who will identify as men.

Regardless of results, research consistently notes that such training—or masculine gender socialization—is generally effective in the reproduction of both an identity people recognize as man and in the creation of new people who see themselves and others as men from generation to generation. As noted at the start of this chapter, even those—like me—who do not conform to the assigned-male-becomes-a-man script experience life constantly aware of and impacted by the ongoing efforts of people to maintain and enforce this script. At the same time, however, recognition of this process of creating and becoming men reveals the malleability of both the identity "man" and beliefs about what it means to become and be a man in society. Throughout this book, my respondents outline how their own experiences being trained to be men necessarily involved violence. In so doing, however, they also reveal that this does not have to be the case, as social authorities and significant others could revise such training programs to transform what it means to be a man in a wide variety of ways.

MEN, MASCULINITY, AND MANHOOD ACTS

To understand both why my respondents' definitions of manhood necessarily included violence and how such notions of what it means to be a man could be changed, however, also requires examining what it means to be a man in U.S. society at present. Put simply, if one is being trained to become a man (instead of a Dreadnought or some other type of being or social identity), we must understand what the contents of these lessons are and how they influence men's reactions to their own and others' actions throughout their lives. Recognizing the importance of this type of analysis, researchers began critically evaluating both men and varied definitions of masculinities more than 40 years ago. In so doing, such efforts have established a massive collection of the ways both men and masculinities are socially constructed and enforced in a wide variety of social settings, populations, locations, and ways over time.[18]

Although reviewing such a large collection of works is a project that itself takes up multiple complete books at present, it is useful here to explore some of the most significant findings that appear throughout this literature. First and foremost, researchers consistently note that what we currently refer to as manhood, or acting in ways that others will see as masculine or otherwise evidence of being a man, is not a physical or personality trait embedded in male bodies. Rather, manhood represents a collective form of practice, belief, and interaction that produces the subordination of women to men, some men to other men, and non-cisgender people (i.e., transgender, non-binary, and gender non-conforming people) to cisgender women and men (especially to cisgender men). In fact, numerous studies have demonstrated how manhood also relies on and reproduces societal patterns of cissexism, endosexism, sexism, monosexism, heterosexism, classism, racism, ageism, nationalism, and religious privilege in the United States. Put simply, existing studies of men and masculinities demonstrate that understanding any large-scale system of inequality in the United States requires interrogating the social construction and enforcement of manhood in society.

To accomplish such interrogation, however, requires analyzing how men signify, or demonstrate to others and themselves, masculine selves (i.e., show that they are men). Following Erving Goffman, [19] this type of work involves the ways men establish and affirm that there is a thing called a man and that such a thing acts in certain ways. Since this type of work can be understood as a performance that people who wish to be seen as men do in order to be recognized as men, Douglas Schrock and Michael Schwalbe argue that we can call such efforts "manhood acts." As they articulate the concept, "manhood acts" are "the identity work males do to claim membership" in the identity category men, "to maintain the social reality of" this category, "to elicit deference from others" within and beyond this category, and "to maintain privileges vis-à-vis women" and other gender groups. [20] Although the contents of a convincing or successful manhood act may vary widely historically, culturally, interpersonally, and locationally, they argue that all manhood acts aim to signify that one is a man by exerting control over others and by resisting being controlled by others throughout their ongoing lives. [21]

To understand which manhood acts will be seen as convincing or successful, however, requires also being aware of the ideal or most respected version of what it means to be a man in a given society, which researchers refer to as "hegemonic masculinity." [22] Although very few people who identify as men will be able to enact the most honored or hegemonic version of manhood in a given space, time, or place, the ideal itself typically carries enough symbolic power to influence the entire culture and provide a yardstick by which all manhood acts may be judged by the performer of them and by others. Goffman, for example, noted:

> In an important sense there is only one unblushing [man] in America: a young, married, white, urban, northern, heterosexual, Protestant father of college education, fully employed, of good complexion, weight, and height, and a recent record in sports. Every American [man] tends to look out upon the world from this perspective. [23]

As such, whenever a person who seeks to be seen by others as a man falls short—even if they only *believe* they fall short—of this ideal, they will likely experience insecurity within their own belief that they have successfully become and are a man.

Building on these insights, researchers have demonstrated that people who identify as men often respond to situations—whether long term or temporary—when they feel like they have fallen short by seeking to compensate for their perceived failure in relation to the hegemonic ideal. At the same time, however, researchers have found many other ways men may feel their identities as men threatened, beyond those outlined by Goffman in the quote above.[24] Put simply, researchers have noted that what may be perceived as a slight or threat to manhood can be as simple as a lack of attention to or recognition of a man's presence nearby and as complex as an ongoing pattern wherein said man's efforts to achieve hegemonic ideals fall even only a little bit short again and again over time (e.g., the person has done well compared to others but feels they have not done well enough or as well as other "real" men). In fact, such patterns have led scholars to argue that every man, at some time and in some way, may need to engage in compensatory behaviors to maintain their sense of themselves as "real" men.

Historically, one way people who identify as men respond to perceived slights or failings in their manhood acts involves imitation of the hegemonic ideal. Since most cultural depictions of manhood are dominated by, identified with, and centered on the most honored way of being a man, this requires acting in ways that affirm the beliefs, values, characteristics, and practices of hegemonic masculinity even when doing so may not be in a given man's best interests. Although this body of scholarship mostly focuses on people who identify as men who do not possess other identities necessary for achieving the hegemonic ideal (e.g., non-heterosexual, non-white), it demonstrates that those who both identify as men and feel unable to enact the hegemonic ideal may engage in "compensatory manhood acts" or attempts to emphasize or exaggerate the hegemonic ideal to signify to themselves and others that they are still men, even when they don't measure up to the dominant version of what it means to be a man.[25]

Throughout this book, I build on this scholarship by examining how violence—whether the threat or enactment of it—may represent a compensatory manhood act, even for men who could enact the hegemonic ideal. Specifically, I outline how men who *could* theoretically enact the hegemonic ideal conceptualize violence as a way of demonstrating manhood in cases where they feel their manhood is questioned, threatened, or slighted in some way. To this end, I explicitly focus on the experiences of people who were assigned male, identify as men, and occupy other social locations (white, heterosexual, college educated, middle- and upper-class) necessary for signifying hegemonic manhood in their own lives. In this way, I argue that one part of combatting violence—and especially men's violence—in society requires detaching violence from what it means to be a man, and in so doing, removing violence as a mechanism whereby men may compensate for perceived loss of status to reassert their own desires to be seen and treated as men by others.

VIOLENCE AS A COMPENSATORY MANHOOD ACT

Although research on compensatory manhood acts typically focuses on people who identify as men who are also members of marginalized groups (e.g., racial or sexual minorities), or are often under the control of organizational or institutional authorities (e.g., treatment centers, prisons), such studies also reveal common factors that lead men to desire and enact compensatory strategies.[26] In the case of members of marginalized groups, for example, experiences with racism, classism, sexism, heterosexism, or other inequalities related to their marginalized identities leads them to report feeling out of control or in need of asserting control or dominance in some other area of their lives. In the case of men in controlled settings, the absence of control over their own lives arises repeatedly in their emphasis on other "manly" behaviors and traits. As Schrock and Schwalbe[27] note in an extensive review of masculinities literatures, the key element of manhood in most cases involves control.

Expanding this observation beyond the cases of men in marginalized groups or controlled settings, it is not difficult to recognize that a large percentage of the situations that make up contemporary social life may leave people who identify as men feeling out of control or controlled by others.[28] If this is the fundamental cause of compensatory manhood acts, then it would not be surprising if men, no matter their standing vis-à-vis elements of the hegemonic ideal, will meet many scenarios wherein such strategies feel right, necessary, and important to their ongoing performance of manhood. This observation represents the central theoretical point of this book: All men will necessarily encounter situations where they are not in control and/or where they are controlled by others. As such, many men will respond to such conditions by using violence, which they were taught was a sign of manhood, to compensate for the perceived slights they experience in such scenarios.

At this point, an example of the way this process plays out may be useful. If, for instance, a man has been taught that he must be sexually desirable to women, he may then make sexual comments to a woman he sees in his daily life. If, however, the woman in question does not respond positively to this action (e.g., she does not affirm the sexual desirability he is supposed to have if he is a man), then he may seek to compensate for his perceived failure to be sexually desirable to women (like men are supposed to be) by verbally, physically, or otherwise attacking the woman in question (calling her derogatory names, following her, etc.). Next, if the woman responds to this violent act in any way, then he can interpret her reaction as evidence of his control over her. The man in question has thus *compensated* for the slight to his manhood (i.e., he is not sexually desirable to this woman) by using violence to re-establish his belief in his own manhood (i.e., he has control over this woman's actions).

Note that in the example above, the man in question could be of any race, class, sex, and age, or of any sexual, religious, or geographic social location. In fact, researchers have demonstrated similar patterns of interaction in settings including but not limited to boardrooms, batterer intervention programs, schools, religious organizations, online platforms, grocery stores, daycare centers, and academic conferences.[29] In all such cases and regardless of the other sociodemographic locations of the man in question, the process is similar. A man seeks to perform a manhood act by demonstrating an element of hegemonic masculinity (in this example, sexual desirability to women), fails to succeed in this performance, and responds with violence of some sort following this failure in order to demonstrate another element of the hegemonic ideal (i.e., using aggression to get fear or attention from others as in the example above). It is this pattern—how violence emerges as a compensatory strategy for people who identify as men—that I focus on throughout this book.

To this end, it is important to note just how common and widespread the pattern noted above is in the existing scientific literature and media concerning gender, violence, and the combination of these areas of study.[30] In terms of locations, for example, researchers have noted (at least implicitly) a similar pattern in settings including but not limited to arcades, construction sites, public streets, churches, schools, families, political rallies, businesses, sports arenas, and media depictions of men and women. Similarly, in terms of violence, researchers have noted similar patterns, including but not limited to domestic battery, bullying, rape and sexual assault, hate crimes, mass shootings and broader gun violence, street harassment, state-sanctioned violence, sexual harassment in the workplace, and murder and manslaughter cases. In all such cases, variations on the same pattern repeat, wherein (1) there are people who were taught they should always be in control; (2) those people, quite naturally, experience many social moments where they are not in control; and (3) many of these people respond to moments when they are not in control by utilizing violence to restore the feeling of control in their own lives and over other people.

THE STUDY

Building on the insights and patterns noted above, this book examines processes whereby people who identify as men may utilize violence as a compensatory manhood act. Specifically, I utilize the statements of my interview respondents, alongside examples from my own life and existing men and masculinities literatures, to note the ways men learn to conceptualize violence as part of what it means to be a man and as a way to re-establish claims to manhood in the face of perceived challenges or threats to their masculinity. In so doing, I argue that an important part of combatting violence in society involves revising contemporary societal definitions of what it means to be a man and the element of violence embedded in such definitions. To this end, I utilize examples in which people who identify as men make sense of violence, manhood, and current gender issues in U.S. political debates. In so doing, I demonstrate how their own notions of violence and manhood fuel reactions to attempts by others to challenge existing gendered, racial, and sexual inequalities in the United States.

At the same time, this study furthers existing work on men, masculinities, and manhood acts by explicitly connecting such work to criminological and other research concerning violence in the United States. I do this by combining examinations of what it means to be a man with analyses of the ways people who identify as men respond to specific issues concerning violence in society at present.[31] Specifically, my work here provides an illustration of the ways people who identify as men make sense of and respond to pressing societal issues, including movements for racial, women's, and LGBT rights; gun violence and mass shootings; domestic violence and sexual assault; and what it means to be a given type of gender in the first place. As such, this work represents a synthesis of prominent topics in gender studies, criminological studies, and current political and policy debates at the intersection of these fields. It is my hope that it will serve as a model for integrating research, advocacy, and discussion on these issues in the future. Even more so, however, I hope readers will take the opportunity to consider what my respondents' examples say about violence and what it means to be a man in contemporary U.S. society with the goal of facilitating discussions and possibilities for change in the nation.

To this end, I utilize autoethnographic data from my own life and an original in-depth interview study, which contains interviews with 50 people who identify as white, cisgender, heterosexual, middle- or upper-class men.[32] My work here offers a rare, in-depth interview study with this population concerning aspects of violence and movements for minority rights in contemporary U.S. society and further provides one of the first occasions wherein contemporary U.S. men react to and make sense of current #MeToo, Black Lives Matter, and Transgender Rights movements that challenge core aspects of their own identities. I thus utilize patterns in these data to capture a portrait of what it means to be a man by people who both identify as men and occupy other socially privileged identity groups and what role violence plays in such meanings as an element of responding to perceived threats to manhood itself.

I focus specifically on men who also occupy privileged racial, class, and sexual social locations to facilitate future discussion and consideration of three interrelated aspects of U.S. society and relationships between violence and manhood. First, I seek to direct attention to the ways that even men who would theoretically be most likely to fit the hegemonic ideal may enact compensatory manhood acts as a result of any occasion where they experience perceived marginalization in society (even if these instances are temporary). Next, I seek to outline the ways that, rather than an exception, violence is defined as an essential element for people who seek to identify as men and be seen as men by others. Finally, I offer a demonstration of the ways these patterns play out in both religious and non-religious[33] men's interpretations of what it means to be a man and what violence has to do with manhood itself.

ORGANIZATION OF THE BOOK

As noted throughout this introduction, manhood, as well as gender more broadly, may be constructed, defined, and performed in a wide variety of ways. At the same time, people hold many different beliefs about what it means to be a member of a given gender group. I thus utilize chapter 2 to contextualize the gender beliefs and attitudes of my interview subjects. Specifically, I explore their own definitions of what it means to be a man as well as what it means to be "other men" or a member of another gender group. In so doing, the chapter allows readers to understand the gender beliefs and attitudes of my subjects to provide a foundation for the chapters on specific aspects of violence and manhood to follow.

After contextualizing the gendered and other beliefs and attitudes of my respondents, chapter 3 turns to the ways they react to and explain violence in contemporary U.S. society. Specifically, I examine how they make sense of violence in their own lives and society through mobilizing excuses for such activities. In so doing, I outline how they both define violence as inevitable and, at the same time, draw a symbolic line between intentional, real violence other men do and accidents that just happen as part of life. I further note how their excuses rely upon societal and personal convictions concerning appropriate expectations and behavior for men in society. Finally, I explore how their efforts to excuse violence allow them to both claim they are not the problem and avoid taking responsibility for changing patterns of violence in the United States.

Especially as gun violence has become a regular and prominent component of U.S. media in recent decades, chapter 4 turns to discussions of this phenomenon. Specifically, I examine how my respondents interpret guns in the United States and the role guns play in their construction of what it means to be a man. To this end, I outline the ways they construct guns as a symbolic demonstration of power, control, and aggression necessary for real manhood.

Then, I examine how both media depictions and my respondents' explanation of reasons for mass shootings and other gun violence mirror components of their definitions of manhood and the compensatory manhood acts people may engage in to repair threatened masculinity. Finally, I outline how their reliance on symbolic notions of guns as a signifier of power and control influence their opinions on gun control and other gun-related policies in the United States.

In chapter 5, I continue looking at specific topics by examining the ways my respondents conceptualized and made sense of sexual violence in society. Specifically, the chapter addresses how they define and construct heterosexuality itself as a form of potential violence. As such, I outline the ways their interpretations of sexualities represent a game wherein heterosexual potential equates to confirmation of manhood and the ways their own sexual activities, stories, and opinions represent compensatory actions by which they seek to avoid feeling insecure about their status as men by dominating or otherwise sexually controlling others. Finally, I discuss how these beliefs define sexual activities in terms that justify the enactment of rape, sexual violence more broadly, and relationships predicated upon domestic violence. In so doing, I demonstrate how their opinions on such topics mirror their own definitions of these topics as part of normal masculine sexual behavior.

Considering the rise of movements and campaigns seeking to combat men's violence in recent years, chapter 6 turns to the ways in which men respond to such efforts. Specifically, I detail how my respondents interpret movements for gendered, sexual, and/or racial justice in the United States. First, I outline how they defined #MeToo as an attack on manhood and argued that it was the real source of gender problems in today's United States. Further, I examine how they negotiate whiteness in their reactions to the Black Lives Matter movement. Specifically, they argue each of these movements are threats to what it means to be a man and how men and other groups are supposed to act in society. Finally, I discuss the ways their conceptualizations of these movements suggest they may see any minority movement as threats that call for them to protect themselves, and manhood itself, over time.

Taken together, these chapters demonstrate the ways violence has been embedded in definitions of what it means to be a man and the ways men respond to movements seeking to curb or lessen violence in the United States. In the final chapter, I outline the ways my respondents' constructions of manhood, violence, and challenges to either reveal how violence operates as a way for men to compensate for perceived slights or threats to their identity claims and privileges as a social group. As such, I argue that fostering less violence and more equitable social relations requires unpacking and transforming what it means to be a man and the ways violence has become part of that definition. In closing, I outline some ways groups seeking more equitable social relations can interrogate and respond to the construction and enactment of violent manhood by problematizing definitions of what it means to be a man in U.S. society.

NOTES

1. For further elaboration and examples of my autoethnographic writing about sexualities, gender, violence, and health over time, see Nowakowski and Sumerau, "Out of the Shadows"; Nowakowski and Sumerau, "Aging Partners Managing Chronic Illness Together"; Nowakowski and Sumerau, "Reframing Health and Illness"; Nowakowski and Sumerau, "Should We Talk about the Pain?"; Sumerau, "I See Monsters"; Sumerau, "Embodying Nonexistence"; and Sumerau and Mathers, *America through Transgender Eyes*. See also my posts on the academic blog www.writewhereithurts.net, such as Sumerau, "Experiencing Gender Variation."

2. I use this term because, due to pervasive cisnormativity in society (i.e., a social world wherein people are taught to see only cisgender women and men), people are trained to only see cisgender people and thus often read others as members of cisgender groups whether the said others ever identify in such a way themselves. Thus, although I do not identify as a man, people may read me or interpret me as such based on their determination of what it means to be a man in a cisgender social order (see also West and Zimmerman, "Doing Gender").

3. For background in these research areas see, for example, Connell, "Doing, Undoing, or Redoing Gender?"; Connell and Messerschmidt, "Hegemonic Masculinity"; Goffman, "The Arrangement between the Sexes"; Moon, Tobin, and Sumerau, "Alpha, Omega, and the Letters in Between"; Ridgeway, *Framed by Gender*; West and Fenstermaker, "Doing Difference"; and West and Zimmerman, "Doing Gender."

4. For discussion of this element in the social sciences and humanities, see Butler, *Gender Trouble*; Serano, *Whipping Girl*; and Smith, *The Everyday World as Problematic*. For such discussion in the physical sciences, see Fausto-Sterling, *Sexing the Body*.

5. For my scholarship to date on men and masculinities, see Cragun and Sumerau, "No One Expects a Transgender Jew"; Cragun and Sumerau, "Men Who Hold More Egalitarian Attitudes"; Sumerau, "That's What a Man Is Supposed to Do"; Sumerau, Barringer, and Cragun, "I Don't Need a Shotgun"; Sumerau, Cragun, and Mathers, "Contemporary Religion and the Cisgendering of Reality"; Sumerau, Cragun, and Mathers, "I Found God in the Glory Hole"; Sumerau, Cragun, and Smith, "Men Never Cry"; Sumerau, Padavic, and Schrock, "Little Girls Unwilling to Do What's Best." For reviews and collections of other scholarship on men and masculinities see, for example, Connell, *Gender and Power*; Connell, *Masculinities*; Connell, *The Men and the Boys*; Connell and Messerschmidt, "Hegemonic Masculinity"; Pascoe and Bridges, *Exploring Masculinities*; Schrock and Padavic, "Negotiating Hegemonic Masculinity"; and Schrock and Schwalbe, "Men, Masculinity, and Manhood Acts."

6. For work on the social production of what we call manhood or masculinities, see, for example, Barber and Bridges, "Marketing Manhood in a 'Post-Feminist' Age"; Carrigan, Connell, and Lee, "Toward a New Sociology of Masculinity"; Connell, *Gender and Power*; Connell, *Masculinities*; Connell, *The Men and the Boys*; Connell and Messerschmidt, "Hegemonic Masculinity"; Eastman and Schrock, "Southern Rock Musicians' Construction of White Trash"; Evans and Davies, "No Sissy Boys Here"; Ezzell, "I'm in Control"; Ezzell, "Pornography, Lad Mags, Video Games, and Boys"; Ferguson, *Bad Boys*; Goffman, "The Arrangement"; Johnson, *The Gender Knot*; Linneman, "How Do You Solve a Problem Like Will Truman?"; Martin, "Mobilizing Masculinities"; Martin, "'Said and Done' versus 'Saying and Doing'"; Messerschmidt, "Becoming 'Real Men'"; Messner, "Boyhood, Organized Sports, and the Construction of Masculinities"; Messner, *Out of Play*; Messner, *Power at Play*; Pascoe, *Dude, You're a Fag*; Pascoe and Bridges, *Exploring Masculinities*; Prokos and Padavic, "There Oughtta Be a Law against Bitches"; Schrock and Padavic, "Negotiating Hegemonic Masculinity"; Schrock and Schwalbe, "Men, Masculinity, and Manhood Acts"; and West and Zimmerman, "Doing Gender."

7. See also Acker, "Inequality Regimes"; Buggs, "(Dis)Owning Exotic"; Buggs, "Does (Mixed-)Race Matter?"; Butler, *Gender Trouble*; Collins, *Black Feminist Thought*; Collins, *Black Sexual Politics*; Crenshaw, "Mapping the Margins"; Martin, "Gender as a Social Institution"; Padavic and Reskin, *Women and Men at Work*; Ridgeway, *Framed by Gender*; Serano, *Whipping Girl*; and Sumerau and Mathers, *America through Transgender Eyes*.

8. For discussion on the "becoming" of identities that exist within a given social world, and the processes whereby people draw on existing cultural archetypes to fashion identities, see Berger and Luckmann, *The Social Construction of Reality*; Garfinkel, *Studies in Ethnomethodology*; Goffman, *Frame Analysis*; Goffman, *Interaction Ritual*; Goffman, *The Presentation of Self in Everyday Life*; Loseke, "The Study of Identity"; McCall and Simmons, *Identities and Interactions*; and Schwalbe and Mason-Schrock, "Identity Work as Group Process."

9. For reviews of this literature, see, for example, Schrock, Sumerau, and Ueno, "Sexualities"; Schwalbe and Mason-Schrock, "Identity Work"; and Wolkomir, *Be Not Deceived*.

10. For those unfamiliar with this reference, Dreadnought is a transgender superheroine and Harry Potter type of character in a young adult series of novels by April Daniels. She is also someone trans girls and women like myself may look up to and emulate and admire, like many people do with other superhero or fantasy characters. I could have utilized any number of characters from literature that children and adults emulate in the formation of identities (e.g., Harry Potter, religious figures in books deemed sacred by a given tradition, Superman), but I chose this one specifically as it is a character people like me admire and emulate but is less known to cisgender audiences.

11. For examples from this literature, see Smith and Cragun, "Mapping Religion's Other"; Sumerau and Cragun, "I Think Some People Need Religion"; Zuckerman, "Atheism, Secularity, and Well-Being"; and Zuckerman, *Living the Secular Life*.

12. For the importance and relative absence of the topic of sex construction and assignment processes in society, see, for example, Davis, *Contesting Intersex*; Karkazis, *Fixing Sex*; Simula, Sumerau, and Miller, *Expanding the Rainbow*; and Sumerau and Mathers, *America through Transgender Eyes*.

13. See again Pascoe and Bridges, *Exploring Masculinities*.

14. See Sumerau, Barringer, and Cragun, "I Don't Need a Shotgun," for discussion of such scripts and representations in society.

15. See again Schrock and Schwalbe, "Men, Masculinity, and Manhood Acts," and Sumerau and Mathers, *America through Transgender Eyes*, for discussion on this point.

16. West and Zimmerman, "Doing Gender"; see also Garfinkel, *Studies in Ethnomethodology*; Goffman, "The Arrangement"; Moon, Tobin, and Sumerau, "Alpha, Omega"; and Ridgeway, *Framed by Gender*.

17. Thorne, *Gender Play*; see also Pascoe, *Dude, You're a Fag*.

18. See again Pascoe and Bridges, *Exploring Masculinities*, and Schrock and Schwalbe, "Men, Masculinity, and Manhood Acts," for reviews of this literature. See also the sources in notes 5, 6, and 7.

19. Goffman, "The Arrangement."

20. Schrock and Schwalbe, "Men, Masculinity, and Manhood Acts," p. 289.

21. See also Ezzell, "I'm in Control"; Schrock, McCabe, and Vaccaro, "Narrative Manhood Acts"; Sumerau, "That's What a Man"; and Sumerau, Padavic, and Schrock, "Little Girls," for more examples.

22. See again Connell and Messerschmidt, "Hegemonic Masculinity"; Schrock and Schwalbe, "Men, Masculinity, and Manhood Acts"; Sumerau, "That's What a Man."

23. Goffman, *Stigma*, p. 128.

24. See, for example, Sumerau, "That's What a Man"; Sumerau, Barringer, and Cragun, "I Don't Need a Shotgun"; and Sumerau, Cragun, and Smith, "Men Never Cry."

25. Sumerau, "That's What a Man."

26. See Anderson, *Code of the Street*; Ezzell, "I'm in Control"; Lee, *Blowin' Up*; and Sumerau, "That's What a Man," for reviews and examples.

27. Schrock and Schwalbe, "Men, Masculinity, and Manhood Acts."

28. See Adams, *Narrating the Closet*; Goffman, *Frame Analysis*; Goffman, *Interaction Ritual*; Goffman, *Presentation of Self*; Goffman, *Stigma*; Lee, *Blowin' Up*; Martin, "Mobilizing

Masculinities"; Mathers, "Bathrooms, Boundaries, and Emotional Burdens"; Schrock and Schwalbe, "Men, Masculinity, and Manhood Acts"; Schrock, Sumerau, and Ueno, "Sexualities"; Sumerau, "Embodying Nonexistence"; Sumerau, "I See Monsters"; and Sumerau, "That's What a Man," for similar observations in specific contexts of everyday social life.

29. For examples and reviews, see Acker, "Inequality Regimes"; Cottom, *Lower Ed*; Dellinger, "Masculinities in 'Safe' and 'Embattled' Organizations"; Ezzell, "I'm in Control"; Martin, *Rape Work*; Ridgeway, *Framed by Gender*; Schilt and Westbrook, "Doing Gender, Doing Heteronormativity"; Schrock and Schwalbe, "Men, Masculinity, and Manhood Acts"; Schwalbe, Godwin, Holden, Schrock, Thompson, and Wolkomir, "Generic Processes in the Reproduction of Inequality"; West and Zimmerman, "Doing Gender"; and Westbrook and Schilt, "Doing Gender, Determining Gender."

30. See, for example, Boyle, "Sexual Assault and Identity Disruption"; Branch and Richards, "The Effects of Receiving a Rape Disclosure"; Browne and Williams, "Gender, Intimacy, and Lethal Violence"; Corzine and Huff-Corzine, "Racial Inequality and Black Homicide"; Dellinger, "Masculinities in 'Safe'"; Garland, Branch, and Grimes, "Blurring the Lines"; Garland, Policastro, Branch, and Henderson, "Bruised and Battered"; Huff-Corzine, Sacra, Corzine, and Rados, "Florida's Task Force Approach to Combat Human Trafficking"; Lanier and Huff-Corzine, "American Indian Homicide"; Martin, "Mobilizing Masculinities"; Martin, *Rape Work*; Navarro and Jasinski, "Going Cyber"; Prokos and Padavic, "An Examination of the Competing Explanations for the Pay Gap"; Richards and Branch, "The Relationship between Social Support and Adolescent Dating Violence"; and Taylor and Jasinski, "Femicide and the Feminist Perspective."

31. At present, these fields often operate in isolation from one another, but at the same time they often speak to similar patterns in criminological (see note 30 for examples) and gender studies (see note 6 for examples), terms, and theoretical debates.

32. See the methodological appendix for more information.

33. The men I interviewed were equally split (25 each) on religious/non-religious identification.

Chapter Two

Defining Manhood

I think about clothing a lot, but it has nothing to do with fashion most of the time. Rather, I think about how the clothes I'm wearing at a given time will impact the ways I will have to navigate other people.[1] When I am at the few places I consider home, for example, I prefer to wear "women's clothes"[2] like so many other women and femme people do, and I don't think much about just how obviously or visibly feminine a given outfit is beyond wondering if I look nice in it. However, much of life requires leaving my homes, and these are the times when clothing becomes a life-or-death decision for me and many other people in the world. When going to the corner store to get some drinks yesterday afternoon, for example, I consciously put on "men's" athletic shorts over my shorter, much more preferable "women's shorts" because while I might get funny looks directed at my long hair or body language wearing the former, I know from too much experience that I might have to survive or avoid a physical altercation if I wear the latter. In either case, things might instead go off without any issues, but I have to be ready for times when issues do arise as I select the outfit in the first place.

These calculations run through my mind each time I get dressed to go outside one of my homes. If I go to work looking like what other people define as a man, I will likely deal with some funny looks or other minor inconveniences as a result of my "feminine" behaviors and body language. If, on the other hand, I wear something too obviously "women's," I may get stopped again for "looking suspicious" or have a bottle or other item thrown at my head. If I wear a skirt underneath my, at least potentially, masculine jeans,[3] I often face a completely different world from the one I meet when the skirt is visible to others. No matter how I dress, I see a woman when I look at myself, and the people close to me see the same. The problems arise, however, in the ways other people define what a man, woman, or any gender should look like and respond to perceived violations of these rules.

The examples above speak to what Laurel Westbrook and Kristen Schilt[4] refer to as processes of "determining gender" that play out throughout social life. In simple terms, people utilize the definitions of gender they have been exposed to and have internalized as real or truthful to determine what gender other people are and should be in daily life. When said people encounter someone who matches their definition of what it means to be a gendered being, the process runs smoothly and they respond to the person as they have been trained to treat people of varied gender identities. At the same time, however, when said people encounter someone who does not match their definitions of what it means to be a given gender,[5] conflict emerges as they seek to make sense of the violation of their beliefs in the moment. Regardless of how this process plays out in millions of interactions every day across the world, it relies on viewing the appearance and behavior of ourselves and others in relation to what definitions of gender we have received.

This is because, as symbolic interactionists have long noted,[6] people typically act and react to other people, ideas, and objects based on the meaning or definition they already have for such people, ideas, and objects. If one has been taught that "a man looks and dresses like this," then one will respond to "this look or dress" as if it is "a man."[7] However, if one encounters a person who does not dress or look like a man is supposed to—based on a definition of what a man is or looks like—one will respond to that look or dress as if it is another identity (woman, non-binary, etc.) that one has been taught exists in the world, or with surprise and conflict when one cannot "determine" which category said person is supposed to fit into based on one's view of the world and how it operates.[8] As such, the meanings or definitions of what it means to be a man or other gendered being shape how a given person will respond to a given gendered other.

For these reasons, it is important to begin our discussion of the relationship between manhood and violence by examining how people who identify as men define what it means to be a man. In this chapter, I examine this topic by sharing the ways the men I interviewed defined what it means to be a man. Further, I juxtapose these constructions of manhood against the ways my respondents defined what it means to be "other men" or members of another gender group. In so doing, this chapter outlines the fundamental gender definitions, or frames,[9] through which my respondents make sense of manhood and gender relations throughout their lives and in relation to other social groups and political conflicts.

GENDERED IDENTITY WORK

To understand how people define what it means to be a man, we must first recognize that "man" is a socially constructed identity that can mean a wide variety of things in different times, places, and populations. [10] Rather than an immutable part of social, psychological, or biological personhood that has remained static throughout history, what it means to be a man shifts and changes over time based on the ways people construct and revise the term. [11] Like all other identities, [12] "man" is thus a meaning people create to explain some aspect of themselves or others in relation to the existing biological, psychological, and social norms of a given time and space. As such, identities themselves are things people can adopt from the wider society but also things people can work on, change, and adjust in relation to a wide variety of factors, available symbolic and material resources, and beliefs available in any given sociocultural context or setting. [13] Put simply, people can work on their identities.

Identity work refers to the efforts people engage in, individually and collectively, to give meaning to themselves and others. Following Schwalbe and Douglas Mason-Schrock, [14] identity work generally involves (1) defining an identity into existence; (2) coding what behaviors, appearances, beliefs, and rituals should be seen or determined as evidence for the defined identity; (3) affirming the performance of these codes to convince self and others that the defined identity is real and accurate; and (4) policing what will or will not be allowed for one who claims to have the defined identity. The combination of these processes will create and define the contours of a given identity claim (e.g., I am a mechanic, mother, white person, bisexual, comic book collector, shortstop, Baptist, working-class person). In fact, researchers have outlined these processes in the creation, maintenance, and adjustment of a wide variety of identity claims in a wide variety of settings over the past four decades. [15]

Especially for people who have never thought about identities in this manner, it may be useful to offer an illustration. Let's assume we have created a new club that we wish to be recognized by others in our life. First, we must define what it means to be a member of this club. For example, we could name ourselves the "muffers" and define a muffer as a member of our new club. Once we have a basic label and definition, we must then establish codes of conduct for muffers. For example, we could decide that muffers (1) attend meetings on Thursday afternoons; (2) express and believe in a universal purpose and merit of human existence; (3) wear purple every Thursday, at meetings, and when doing volunteer work; and (4) volunteer at food banks every weekend. Now, we have behaviors we can do to tell ourselves and others we are muffers and members of our new club.

Next, we find occasions to affirm these behaviors as "what muffers do." Thus, we repeat these behaviors in meetings, get attention for them from others, and react positively when our fellow members engage in these behaviors. This affirmation will allow each of us to believe in our new identities as muffers and tell potential new members how to become a muffer. Finally, we must establish boundaries around our new identities, which will allow us to say what muffers are not. This is because other people might meet on Thursdays, share our beliefs in purpose and merit, wear purple at the same times we do, and volunteer at food banks on weekends. As such, we create a rule that "muffers are required to attend Thursday events every week and must always wear a specific purple logo when they can." We now have a way to say these are the muffers (i.e., those who follow the new rule), but other people doing similar things are not muffers (i.e., those who are not part of our club). In this way, we have created an identity—a person may learn to be and be seen by others as a muffer.

Although the above example is hypothetical, we can see these processes playing out at present where new groups or even populations become more visible in mainstream society. After establishing the terms genderqueer and non-binary in the 1990s, for example, people who utilize these identity terms defined non-binary as people who are neither men nor women in terms of gender. Currently, many behaviors are being proposed regarding what it means to be, look, behave, and otherwise be seen as a non-binary person. At the same time, many groups have emerged online and offline for people to find others who affirm their non-binary identities and performance of non-binary dress, behavior, and other activity. Finally, we already see debates emerging as to what counts as non-binary, genderqueer, agender, all of these identities or just some of these identities, and what does not count in each or all of these groups.[16] Whether we look to the hypothetical example or an example like non-binary occurring around us at present, we see the processes whereby people create and establish the contours of a given identity claim they may identify with and find recognition of from others in the course of their lives.

Since identity work is always in progress,[17] researchers have spent considerable time demonstrating the ways people utilize the symbolic and material resources at their disposal to tell themselves and others who they are, who they are not, and who they believe others to be. As suggested at the beginning of this chapter, people may do this with their appearance by dressing in specific ways (e.g., football fans wear this type of clothing), displaying specific symbols (e.g., this necklace relates to that religion), or otherwise symbolizing their identities to others who may or may not recognize the symbols. People may also do this by interpreting behaviors as evidence of a given identity (e.g., black people act like this; hockey fans act like this). In fact, researchers have demonstrated that any aspect of a given society can be mobilized in the service of a given set of identity claims. As such, much attention has been granted to the ways this is done and the specific definitions of identities that given groups establish and maintain over time.

In fact, this type of research lies at the heart of much of the gender scholarship that undergirds the analyses throughout this book. Specifically, researchers have examined the historical creation of gender categories and identities throughout the world.[18] They have further outlined the multitude of ways people define themselves and others as members of a given gender group in everyday interactions, surveys, religious traditions, families, legal documentation, schools, and every other setting of contemporary social life.[19] They have also outlined how people's beliefs concerning what constitutes masculine, feminine, and androgynous behaviors and identities facilitate differential treatment of people within such settings.[20] Such research also demonstrates how sex categorization influences and then becomes a type of evidence for beliefs about particular behaviors and attitudes people may have if they identify with a specific gendered identity or population.[21] The combination of such work demonstrates that gendered identity work permeates every aspect of contemporary societies.

As Cecelia Ridgeway notes in her analysis of these dynamics in varied work and familial settings,[22] many of these endeavors emerge from the ways almost every aspect of social life is framed or defined as evidence of a given gender. Such framing, in the education and training of each new generation of humans, facilitates expectations about gender that find voice in social life when people (1) seek to live their own lives and genders based on such expectations, and/or (2) face others (or have experiences) that violate such expectations in the empirical world. As Ridgeway notes, the combination of social phenomena defined as evidence of a given gender and expectations that such definitions are accurate facilitate many of the ways people understand themselves and interact with others across settings. Stated another way, people are generally taught there is a way "this gender" looks, acts, and thinks, and then they learn to have these expectations about gender throughout their interactions with others.

These expectations create a social life predicated on an if/then test that West and Zimmerman refer to as "doing gender."[23] Put simply, they argue that people experience social life in its entirety as an effort to do (or perform or practice) gendered beliefs they have been taught while holding others accountable to the same beliefs. As such, most people move through their daily lives, consciously or not, repeating the same set of mental calculations. If, for example, I see someone with long hair wearing tight clothes, then I may assume this person is feminine or a woman and treat them according to the beliefs I have been taught about how one should treat women or feminine people. In this way, most people move through life, as Ridgeway puts it,[24] framing themselves and others based on whatever gender beliefs they have learned and expecting themselves and others to do or accomplish behaviors that match these beliefs. When people do not behave in ways that match these beliefs, however, then they must be held accountable (i.e., confronted) and made to answer for their violation of the ways gender is supposed to be done and defined by others.

As noted previously, Westbrook and Schilt[25] extend these ideas by focusing attention on the ways people draw upon both (1) how gender has been defined or framed for them, and (2) how they do and expect others to do gender to (3) determine the gender of others. If someone determines that another person is a man, for example, they will seek to hold that person accountable to what it means to be a man based on their beliefs about who and how men are. This may escape notice if the person in question does gender based on the ways one should act as a man, but it will lead to conflict instead if the person in question does *not* do gender in the ways one should as a man. In that case, the original someone must either (1) revise their determination of gender or (2) ignore or seek to punish the violation of their determination of gender. Although the person in question may choose the former option and revise their expectations, it is more common that they will engage in the latter option and seek to re-establish (or affirm) their definitions of gender, how one should do gender, and how to determine gender.

In fact, studies of transgender experience demonstrate these processes occurring throughout contemporary social settings.[26] When transgender people are determined by others to be in line with the expectations of cisgender womanhood and manhood, for example, they are often treated in similar ways to cisgender women and men. At other times, transgender people whom others determine to be somewhere between mainstream or normative expectations for manhood and womanhood are generally met with different reactions. In some cases, they are embraced by others as the gender with which they claim, and these others, whether cisgender, transgender, or anywhere in between, revise their expectations in the process. In many cases, however, transgender people are subjected to harassment and other negative treatment as mostly cisgender others seek to maintain their beliefs in a world of only cisgender people who conform to normative notions of cisgender womanhood and manhood. In such cases, the processes of defining, doing, and determining gender occurring throughout society become more visible because people encounter others who do not fit into their gendered expectations.

It is these expectations that I focus on in this chapter. Specifically, the following sections outline what my respondents say it means to be a man, and what it means to be "other men" or a member of another gender group. In so doing, they outline the definitions that guide their own efforts to do and determine the gender of themselves and others throughout their lives. As I argue in later chapters, these fundamental notions of gender find voice in their responses to contemporary political debates. Further, as I show here and throughout this book, violence—or at least the potential for it—permeates their fundamental notions of what it means to be a man in the United States at present, as well as the ways my respondents make sense of others in the social world.

WHAT IT MEANS TO BE A MAN

Throughout this book, I utilize the statements of people who identify as men and who are also capable of enacting hegemonic masculinity to demonstrate the fundamental role violence (or at least the ever-present possibility of it) plays in the social construction of contemporary manhood. To this end, it is important to note that the men I interviewed are also in the most privileged social groups in terms of race (white men), sex (assigned male cisgender men), sexuality (heterosexual men), and class (middle- and upper-class men). They are also all young (between the ages of 18 and 24 years old) and college educated to an extent (they were all in college or just completing college at the time of the interview).[27] Existing masculinities studies would thus suggest the men whose statements provide the basis for this book would be the most capable of reaching the hegemonic ideal of what it means to be a man as well as the least likely to need to engage in strategies to compensate for perceived slights and challenges to their identities as men.[28]

However, the men interviewed for this study did differ in terms of religious beliefs. Half of the respondents identify as religious men (25), and the other half identify as non-religious men (25). I took this approach because research is mixed on the status of religious identity vis-à-vis the hegemonic ideal.[29] Some studies dating back to at least the 1960s suggest that religious, and especially Christian, status is necessary for enacting ideal manhood in the United States.[30] At the same time, recent years have witnessed growing numbers of people identifying as non-religious as well as the emergence of explicitly non-religious movements that are predominately composed of cisgender, heterosexual, middle- and upper-middle-class white men.[31] Although these groups of men differ in their opinions about the supernatural, they share much by way of demographics and socialization. Following Jennifer Dunn and S. J. Creek,[32] I sought to investigate to what extent they differed or aligned in their beliefs about gender. I discuss these comparisons where relevant throughout the analyses in this book.

I begin such analyses by exploring how the men I interviewed defined what it means to be a man. As prior research suggests,[33] they often began their own elaborations of what constitutes a man with discussions about sex assignment. Religious men, as evidenced in the following quote from a 22-year-old Christian man I call Mark,[34] appealed to notions of God-given biology: "Well, a man is just a male, it's really that simple. God created male and female, and he created males to be men." Likewise, non-religious men, as evidenced by the following statement from a 21-year-old atheist man I call Harry, inserted nature in the place of God to offer the same opinion: "It's just nature, we are all born men or women, and that's it. When you're born a male, you're a man." Most of the respondents, regardless of religion or age, offered similar statements at some point in the interview. In such cases, men were made by God or nature as the automatic extension of male bodies.

Interestingly, even when the men I interviewed initially said it was "just God's design" or "just simple biology," they would quickly revise their statements to explain that "it isn't just about being male" when I asked them about trans men or people with intersex bodies.[35] In such cases, as illustrated by the following comments from a 20-year-old religious[36] man I call Brad, maleness was not enough to be considered a man:

> Well, I didn't really mean it was just about being male, I mean, that is part of it, but its more about how you live, I mean, how you carry yourself and that kind of thing. It's more about who you are as a person, I guess that's what I mean. You might not have to be male, right, but you have to understand stuff or see things like a male would, does that make sense? It's like a way of seeing the world, that kind of thing.

As a 20-year-old atheist man I call Roger put it: "It's more of a mindset than just about being male. It's how you see things on a deeper level." Respondents would thus define manhood as an extension of maleness until I pointed out that many men are not born nor ever become "male." Once this possibility was brought into the conversation, they quickly decided that manhood was more complicated than whether or not someone was male.

Seeking to understand this complexity, I would follow these exchanges with probing questions to try to understand what they thought a man was in terms of actions or ways "of seeing things" as a person in society. This did not mean that the men I interviewed did not continue to mention the importance of seemingly male bodies or bodily characteristics. Rather, they did continue to list embodied ways one could signify or present manhood to others including but not limited to being strong, large, hairy, muscular, and/ or in possession of a larger penis. The following statement from a 23-year-old Christian man I call Matthew offers a typical illustration: "Men are just bigger, stronger, and more powerful physically, that's a big part of really being a man, building your body in the right ways." As is common in prior research on embodied masculinity,[37] my respondents linked manhood to the possession of larger bodies capable of exhibiting power, muscular builds, and hair.

At the same time, however, they began to talk about the ways one must act to be considered a man. Especially considering their own social locations within systems of race, sex, and age, it was not surprising that they seemed to be reading from a hegemonic masculinity textbook when sharing such behaviors. As a non-religious 22-year-old man I call Nate put it:

> A man is supposed to be a protector, you protect the people you care about, and you provide for them. Men take care of the people in their lives, that's what it's really about. Men have to be aggressive, strong, and confident because we have to protect the women and children and provide for them too. No matter what else, a man has to do that. He has to be able to put food on the table and make sure nothing bad happens to his family. That's just what a man does so I guess that's what it means to be a real man.

Echoing decades of research on hegemonic manhood, Nate defines manhood in terms of breadwinning (i.e., providing for others and putting food on the table) and defending others from harm (i.e., protecting women and children). This was a common thread running throughout the interviews; men are people who protect others by, for example, providing for them, advising them, or physically (sometimes sexually) taking care of them.

Although they phrased it in different ways, each of the men I spoke with defined manhood by emphasizing the ability to protect the self and others. A Jewish 21-year-old I call Micah, for example, put it this way: "Being a man is, I mean it's a lot of things, but really, it's about being a kind of wall between your people and anything bad." A 22-year-old non-religious man I call Zack echoed this sentiment: "I guess the main thing is protecting the people you care about, that's kind of the main thing. Men are the ones who do that, that's what we do. That's why most of the military and police are men. It's just the way it is." A 19-year-old Christian man I call Bryan added: "The world is nuts, okay, and as men, it's our job to take care of that, to keep that stuff under control, you know, to protect everyone else." A non-religious 23-year-old I call Lenny agreed: "It's all about being a protector, that's what I got from my dad, you provide for your family, and so you protect them from harm no matter the cost." In each case, the men I interviewed conceptualized manhood in terms of protection they could offer.

In some ways, the emphasis on protection throughout the interviews fits prior studies of men and masculinities. Examining decades of such scholarship, Schrock and Schwalbe[38] noted that manhood, in all its varied forms, typically involved the ability to control the self and others and avoid being controlled by others. If manhood refers to someone who protects the self and others from harm, however, then it also means one who has control over whether or not the self or others will be harmed. Especially as men no longer possess the institutional power to automatically control, for example, the economic options, the sexual choices, or the bodily decisions of other gender groups, the construction of themselves as protectors who wield control over potential harms provides a definition of manhood that is not dependent on outperforming other gender groups in other social arenas.

At the same time, however, the construction of men as protectors requires establishing both (1) whom they are protecting, and (2) what they are protecting said people from. Stated another way, if being a man means that one is capable of and responsible for protecting others, then one will need others to protect and dangers to protect others from in order to be a man. As I argue throughout this book, this means that part of being a man (i.e., a protector) means being continuously prepared for at least the possibility of experiencing violence one can try to protect themselves and others from and/or having to dispense violence in order to protect others. In fact, this facet of defining manhood in terms of protection becomes evident when the men I interviewed talk about other people in society.

MEN'S DEFINITIONS OF OTHERS

If men are protectors, two questions automatically come to mind. First, who are they protecting themselves and others from in the first place? For the men I interviewed, the simple answer to this question is other men, but especially men who are defined as dangerous as a result of class and/or racial difference. Second, who do they see as the people they are supposed to protect? In this case, respondents defined women and children as the main groups in need of such protection. Interestingly, religious and non-religious respondents offered the same conceptualizations of women, but they each utilized different rationales for these opinions. In the next section, I explore how they accomplished these endeavors by defining whom they would protect and what they were protecting them from.

Protecting People from Other Men

Although generally focused on the efforts of people who occupy marginalized positions within a given society, researchers have outlined a generic process in the reproduction of inequality referred to as "defensive othering."[39] In simple terms, defensive othering occurs when members of a given group agree with negative stereotypes about their group but suggest they are the exception to those stereotypes. Although the men I interviewed were by no means members of subordinated race, class, sex, sexual, or gender groups, they engaged in a similar process whereby they defined other men as dangerous, predatory, and violent while arguing that real men did not behave this way and instead protected others from such bad men. In so doing, my respondents drew a metaphorical line in the sand between themselves (real men who protect others) and other men (the bad men who harm others).

For example, when I asked a 24-year-old religious man I call Timothy what he thought he should protect others from, he stated: "Well, men of course, but not the good kind of man. There are men who rape and kill and do all kinds. They're not going to stop unless someone stops them, and that's what a real man does, stops them before they can hurt people." A non-religious 22-year-old I call Derek added: "Look, I've been in locker rooms, I know how other guys are, and I don't want that coming back on my girl. Somebody has to protect her from those kinds of guys. That's my job." A 21-year-old non-religious respondent I call Greg echoed many other respondents by stating: "That's what the media misses, man. There are terrible guys out there who just don't care, but real men are the ones protecting everybody else from them." Throughout the interviews, respondents suggested that toxic masculinity and men's violence against women and others were concrete facts, but that the real men were the ones who protected other people from these forms of masculinity, rather than the ones doing such deeds.

The men I interviewed were also concerned with protecting themselves from these other men. A respondent I call Evan, a 19-year-old non-religious man, offered a typical example:

> I grew up with other guys and most of them were assholes. I mean that. The things guys do to each other, just to fit in, it's crazy, man. I even did some bad things. I can admit that. The thing is, when you know those kinds of guys are out there, you know, the crazy guys who just don't care, you also know you have to be ready. You gotta be able to defend yourself because nobody else is going to do it for you, that's just the truth. I know so many guys back home, they just don't care about anything, and that's just wild. I don't want them near me, but I know that I'm ready if they mess with me, and that's important.

For Evan and many other respondents, the experiences they had with other men showed them that men's violence was just something they had to be "ready for" in their lives. Whether or not they admitted to having been similar in the past (and over half did admit this), they explained that they were better than that now, but still needed to be ready to protect themselves from the bad guys. As a 24-year-old non-religious respondent I call Terry put it, "Other men are dangerous, and so you have to become dangerous too just to protect yourself from them."

Although each of my respondents saw themselves as the real men who protected themselves and others, their conceptualization of the other, dangerous men included elements of classism and racism about half the time. Classism, as illustrated by the following quote from a 19-year-old Christian respondent I call Adam, was often expressed by suggesting people from the lower classes were just more violent: "You go into these poor areas where people just don't care about anything and just drink beer and whatever, they're dangerous, they got nothing so they don't care if they get hurt." A non-religious 22-year-old I call Jim added: "I think it's the way some guys are raised. A friend of mine grew up in a trailer park, right, and he said it was just nonstop drama there. The people just act like animals, that sounds bad, but it's just the truth." In these and other statements, some respondents defined the dangerous other men as those in different (and lesser) economic classes who were too poor to be the good men they were.

This same kind of pattern emerged in many of the interviews when, instead of or alongside class differences, respondents defined the dangerous, violent men in terms of racial differences. A 22-year-old Christian respondent I call Barry shared: "You see the news, right? I know it's not polite, but the black guys just have issues, okay. They're more violent, you see it all the time, it's just the way they are, and people just don't want to admit it." A respondent I call Lionel who identified as a 24-year-old atheist added: "You gotta be ready for the illegal immigrants and the gangbangers, that's part of it. Who's gonna protect my sister from them? It's gotta be me, it's that simple." Once again, the "different" dangerous men who my respondents felt the need to protect themselves and others from were not just other men, but often also other men who occupied different racial and class social locations than they do.

Throughout the interviews, men were the people in society that my respondents suggested posed the most danger to others. At the same time, however, these were always *other men*, and often other men from different racial and class populations. Echoing social media hashtags and news programming arguing that "not all men" commit violence, my respondents suggested that other men were the problem and real men, like themselves, were the ones who could protect people from this problem. In both cases, however, the relationship between violence and manhood held firm: Men will engage in violence, and therefore "real" men can, and should always be prepared to, use violence to protect people from these "other" men. Whether as protectors or as the danger to be protected against, respondents implicitly argued that violence was a necessary component of manhood.

Protecting Women and Children

Historically, one of the primary justifications for men's control over women involves arguments that women are the weaker, softer, more vulnerable, or otherwise less independent gender group.[40] The men I interviewed echoed these long-standing concerns when defining manhood in terms of the protection men could offer to others. In fact, as suggested by some of the quotes in the previous section, the others were almost entirely framed as women, though in many cases children were added to these statements as well. This was, however, one case in which religion and non-religion appeared to play roles in the definitional work of these men. Both groups defined women as in need of men's protection, but religious men said this was because of how *God* made women and men, and non-religious men said this was because of the *natural differences* between men and women. As was the case in their responses about maleness, the two groups provided the same answer but utilized different source material to craft their rationale for these beliefs.

For example, a 20-year-old religious respondent I call Donovan offered a statement echoing most of the religious men's comments:

> Our job is to protect women. God made men and women different, not better or worse I would say, but different. Women are just not as strong as men. If some big man wants to hurt them, well, there isn't really anything they can do. That's not their fault, but it makes it even more important for men to do what we're supposed to do.

Similarly, Danny, a 20-year-old atheist, summed up the non-religious men's take on the issue: "We have to protect women because that's just nature—women are more nurturing, but men are stronger and more aggressive, so naturally, we have to look out for them." Whether they used God or nature as their rationale, religious and non-religious men agreed that women needed to be protected because they were less able to do so for themselves.

Variations of the statements above occurred throughout the interviews. In many cases (over half), respondents also mentioned children as a group of people who needed their protection. A religious 22-year-old I call Seth offered a typical example:

> It's about the women and children. My dad was always there to protect us, and that's what I learned from him. A man protects his family from danger. That part is not optional, that's what he would say. "Son," he would say, "you gotta take care of the people who can't take care of themselves because this is a dangerous world and your family is all you really have." That's why I say protection, because a man has to protect what he has, his family, his wife and child.

In such cases, respondents did two things. First, they defined women and children as the people in need of their manly protection. At the same time, however, they also suggested that women and children were possessions rather than people and that part of protecting them involved maintaining the possessions that every man should have in this life. In so doing, respondents, regardless of intentions, reproduced long-standing beliefs about the lesser status of women and children in relation to the men in their lives.

UNDERSTANDING MANHOOD AND VIOLENCE

In this chapter, I outlined how the men I interviewed defined what it means to be a man. Specifically, they define men as protectors who are responsible for keeping others safe and away from harm. In so doing, however, they define other men as the likely source of such harm, and women as a subordinate group in need of men's protection from other men. Further, these conceptualizations of what a man is and does also include racialized and classed assumptions characterizing other men as violent and implicit suggestions that women are possessions that belong to the men who protect them. In all these ways, my respondents' definitions of what it means to be a man suggest that men's violence—as attackers and/or protectors—are inevitable aspects of contemporary manhood in U.S. society.

The suggestion that violence is inevitable creates a situation wherein the men I interviewed accept violence as a natural part of society, but at the same time, they seek to define themselves as the good people who protect others from this endless threat. In the next chapter, I explore this situation by examining how the men I interviewed made sense of violence in the broader society as well as their place in such dynamics. Since their definitions of manhood require violence to be a major part of social life, they do not explicitly oppose violence itself. At the same time, since violence is considered negative or bad in society, they must find ways to agree that it is not a good thing while also maintaining belief in its necessity. As I show in chapter 3, they accomplish this by excusing violence in ways that position themselves as the good ones who may accidentally do violence when they have to and others as the real violent threats who intentionally cause harm to others.

NOTES

1. See Sumerau, "Embodying Nonexistence," for examples; see also Lucal, "What It Means to Be Gendered Me."

2. Here, I refer to clothes labeled and marketed for women and sold in the women's department in stores.

3. I use this phrasing because I generally wear "women's jeans," but jeans seem to look pretty similar to most people—or at least rarely occasion comment—regardless of which section of a given store displays them or what type of sizing is utilized.

4. Westbrook and Schilt, "Doing Gender, Determining Gender."

5. Lucal, "What It Means"; Schrock, "Transsexuals' Narrative Construction of the 'True Self.'"

6. See, for example, Blumer, *Symbolic Interaction*; Dingwall, "Notes toward an Intellectual History"; Fenstermaker, "The Turn from 'What' to 'How'"; Goffman, *Interaction Ritual*; Goffman, *The Presentation of Self in Everyday Life*; Goffman, *Stigma*; Hollander, "I Demand More of People"; and Schwalbe, Godwin, Holden, Schrock, Thompson, and Wolkomir, "Generic Processes in the Reproduction of Inequality."

7. See Dozier, "Beards, Breasts, and Bodies."

8. In fact, one could argue that doing and determining gender are examples of people doing a gendered form of symbolic interaction throughout their everyday lives; see Sumerau, Mathers, and Moon, "Foreclosing Fluidity."

9. Ridgeway, *Framed by Gender.*

10. See, for example, Akihiko and Pih, "Men Who Strike"; Asencio, "'Locas,' Respect, and Masculinity"; Connell, *Gender and Power*; Connell, *Masculinities*; Connell, *The Men and the Boys*; Connell and Messerschmidt, "Hegemonic Masculinity"; Kasim, "Mappila Muslim Masculinities"; Kong, "Be a Responsible and Respectable Man"; Martin, "Mobilizing Masculinities"; McGuire, Berhanu, Davis, and Harper, "In Search of Progressive Black Masculinities"; Mirandé, Pitones, and Díaz, "Quien Es el Mas Macho?"; Pascoe and Bridges, *Exploring Masculinities*; Schrock and Schwalbe, "Men, Masculinity, and Manhood Acts"; and Wingfield, "Racializing the Glass Escalator."

11. For examples in the social scientific literature, see Besen-Cassino, "Gender Threat and Men"; Bridges, "The Costs of Exclusionary Practices"; Cserni and Essig, "Twenty Years of *Men and Masculinities*"; Ekşi, "Police and Masculinities in Transition"; and Emig, "Terrorist Masculinities." For examples beyond this literature, see the films *Tough Guise* and *Tough Guise 2.*

12. Goffman, *Presentation of Self*; Goffman, *Stigma*; McCall and Simmons, *Identities and Interactions*; and Strauss, *Mirrors and Masks.*

13. Ezzell, "Barbie Dolls"; Ezzell, "I'm in Control"; Johnson, *The Gender Knot*; Snow and Anderson, "Identity Work among the Homeless."

14. Schwalbe and Mason-Schrock, "Identity Work as Group Process"; Schwalbe et al., "Generic Processes."

15. For examples, see Acosta, "Cultivating a *Lesbiana Seria* Identity"; Barbee and Schrock, "Un/gendering Social Selves"; Creek, "Not Getting Any"; Garcia, *Respect Yourself, Protect Yourself*; Garrison, "On the Limits of 'Trans Enough'"; Jones, "The Pleasures of Fetishization"; Mathers, "Bathrooms, Boundaries"; Pfeffer, "I Don't Like Passing"; Pitt, "Still Looking for My Jonathan"; Ponticelli, "Crafting Stories"; Reese, "Gendered Identity Work"; and Sumerau, "Somewhere between Evangelical and Queer."

16. Barbee and Schrock, "Un/gendering Social Selves"; Darwin, "Doing Gender beyond the Binary"; Feinberg, *Stone Butch Blues*; Mathers, "Navigating Genderqueer Existence"; Rajunov and Duane, *Nonbinary*; Sumerau and Mathers, *America through Transgender Eyes.*

17. For examples, see note 15.

18. Driskill, Justice, Miranda, and Tatonetti, *Sovereign Erotics*; Samuels, *Fantasies of Identification*; Snorton, *Black on Both Sides*; Somerville, *Queering the Color Line*; Stryker, *Transgender History*; Wesley, "Twin-Spirited Woman."

19. For examples, see Connell, C., "Doing, Undoing, or Redoing Gender?"; Connell, R., "Accountable Conduct"; Darwin, "Doing Gender Beyond"; Lampe, Carter, and Sumerau, "Continuity and Change in Gender Frames"; Mathers, "Bathrooms, Boundaries"; Schilt and Westbrook, "Doing Gender, Doing Heteronormativity"; shuster, "Punctuating Accountability"; Trautner, "Doing Gender, Doing Class"; Vidal-Ortiz, "The Figure of the Transwoman of Color"; West and Zimmerman, "Doing Gender"; Westbrook and Schilt, "Doing Gender, Determining Gender."

20. See Cragun and Sumerau, "The Last Bastion," and Cragun and Sumerau, "No One Expects a Transgender Jew." For a review, see Worthen, "An Argument for Separate Analyses of Attitudes."

21. Costello, "Not a 'Medical Miracle'"; Costello, "Trans and Intersex Children"; Davis, *Contesting Intersex*; Davis, Dewey, and Murphy, "Giving Sex"; Fausto-Sterling, *Sexing the Body*; Karkazis, *Fixing Sex.*

22. Ridgeway, *Framed by Gender.*

23. West and Fenstermaker, "Doing Difference"; West and Zimmerman, "Accounting for Doing Gender"; West and Zimmerman, "Doing Gender."

24. Ridgeway, *Framed by Gender.*

25. Westbrook and Schilt, "Doing Gender, Determining Gender."

26. For examples, see Beemyn and Rankin, *The Lives of Transgender People*; Califia, *Sex Changes*; Castañeda, "Developing Gender"; Davis, *Beyond Trans*; Doan, "To Count or Not to

Count"; Halberstam, *In a Queer Time and Place*; James, Herman, Rankin, Keisling, Mottet, and Anafi, *Report of the 2015 U.S. Transgender Survey*; Jauk, "Gender Violence Revisited"; Johnson, "Normative Accountability"; Lombardi, "Trans Issues in Sociology"; Mathers, "Bathrooms, Boundaries"; Meadow, *Trans Kids*; Miller and Grollman, "The Social Costs of Gender Nonconformity"; Pfeffer, *Queering Families*; Raun, *Out Online*; Rebchook, Keatley, Contreras, Perloff, Molano, Reback, et al., "Transgender Woman of Color Initiative"; Schilt and Lagos, "Development of Transgender Studies"; Schrock, Reid, and Boyd, "Transsexuals' Embodiment of Womanhood"; Snorton, *Black on Both Sides*; Stryker, *Transgender History*; Sumerau and Mathers, *America through Transgender Eyes*; Vidal-Ortiz, "Queering Sexuality and Doing Gender"; zamantakis, "I Try Not to Push It Too Far."

27. See the methodological appendix for more information on the study.

28. Cheng, "Marginalized Masculinities"; Connell, *Gender and Power*; Connell, *Masculinities*; Connell, *The Men and the Boys*; Connell and Messerschmidt, "Hegemonic Masculinity"; Schrock and Schwalbe, "Men, Masculinity, and Manhood Acts"; Sumerau, "That's What a Man."

29. Avishai, "'Doing Religion' in a Secular World"; Burke, *Christians under Covers*; Gerber, "Grit, Guts, and Vanilla Beans"; Moon, *God, Sex, and Politics*; Sumerau, Barringer, and Cragun, "I Don't Need a Shotgun"; Sumerau, Cragun, and Smith, "Men Never Cry"; Wolkomir, *Be Not Deceived*.

30. Aune, "Fatherhood in British Evangelical Christianity"; Gerber, "Grit, Guts"; Goffman, *Stigma*; McDowell, "Aggressive and Loving Men"; Pitt, "Killing the Messenger"; Sumerau, "That's What a Man"; Sumerau, Cragun, and Mathers, "I Found God"; Thumma, "Negotiating a Religious Identity."

31. Cimino and Smith, *Atheist Awakening*; Cimino and Smith, "Secular Humanism and Atheism"; Dunn and Creek, "Identity Dilemmas"; LeDrew, "Discovering Atheism"; Zuckerman, "Atheism, Secularity"; Zuckerman, *Living the Secular Life*.

32. Dunn and Creek, "Identity Dilemmas."

33. Schrock and Schwalbe, "Men, Masculinity, and Manhood Acts."

34. All names for respondents discussed in this book are pseudonyms.

35. For research on transmen see Abelson, *Men in Place*; Cromwell, *Transmen and FTMs*; Currah, "Expecting Bodies"; Johnson, "Transnormativity"; Pfeffer, *Queering Families*; Rogers, *Trans Men in the South*; Rubin, *Self-Made Men*; Schilt, "Just One of the Guys?"; and Vidal-Ortiz, "Queering Sexuality." For research on intersex bodies, see the citations in note 21.

36. I utilize simply "religious" or "non-religious" when the respondent did not specify a particular religious or non-religious tradition or affiliation.

37. Vaccaro, "Male Bodies in Manhood Acts."

38. Schrock and Schwalbe, "Men, Masculinity, and Manhood Acts."

39. Ezzell, "Barbie Dolls"; Schwalbe et al., "Generic Processes."

40. Connell, *Gender and Power*; Martin, "Gender as a Social Institution"; Padavic and Reskin, *Women and Men at Work*.

Chapter Three

Excusing Violence

When I was a small child, I got into my first fistfight. I never learned the name of the (as far as I know) "boy" I fought with that day. He saw me in the woods looking at a pile of scrunchies I snuck out of my adoptive sister's room. I was dreaming of wearing them. I was imagining how each different color would go with my hair. He called me some name I don't remember, threw a rock at me, and lunged at me like he was going to beat me up. I sidestepped him, and the fight began. I don't remember much about it. What I remember is going home covered in mud and a little bit of blood. I remember my adoptive parents asked what happened. I remember I told them that I got in a fight, but I left out the part about the scrunchies. I remember their reaction was mostly positive. It was the first time I heard the phrase "Boys will be boys," and the first time I was congratulated for using violence against another person.

I often think about this event in relation to a different situation a few weeks later when I was caught by my older, but not oldest, adoptive sister playing with a dress. I remember getting yelled at. I don't know if my adoptive parents were told, but I always thought they were, because the next day my adoptive father was angry with me and gave me a talk about being tough for some reason. The events run together in my head because I remember trying to use the same phrase, or excuse, that my adoptive parents used to describe the fistfight. My sister was angry, and I joked that "boys will be boys," but this time, it didn't work. Instead, I got a lecture on the differences between boys and girls. I remember she told me that playing with girls' clothes was inexcusable, a word I didn't really understand at the time and had to look up in the dictionary, and that I was lucky she caught me instead of our parents.

Years later, the thing that stuck with me about the two events was the difference between excusable behavior (e.g., someone my family thought was a boy being violent came equipped with an excuse for anything negative about such an activity) and inexcusable behavior (e.g., someone my family thought was a boy had no excuse for dressing in a way that was not approved for boys). In fact, I would watch this same dynamic play out when, for example, students and friends who were assigned male at birth shared similar experiences about being caught wearing "girls" clothes as children[1] while at the same time the nation watched media, pundits, voters, and celebrities practically bend over backwards to excuse violence, harassment, and bullying by celebrities, politicians, and others across the nation.[2] My family and the nation were always ready, it seemed, to excuse the violent behavior of those considered boys and men but were just as ready to denounce and attack any example of gender non-conformity by people assigned male at birth who might or might not have ever identified as men themselves.

These dynamics, in my life and in our current sociopolitical culture as a nation, reflect patterns in the literature on the maintenance of social norms, and the processes whereby people excuse and justify some forms of activity (what is perceived as normal in a given social context) while denouncing other forms of activity (what is perceived as abnormal in a given social context).[3] Following Marvin Scott and Stanford Lyman,[4] such endeavors rely on people mobilizing accounts (or recognizable stories) that excuse or justify some types of action that are socially defined as normal, natural, and inevitable in a given social context while also maintaining said norms by attacking any types of action deemed outside such norms, nature, or inevitability. In so doing, people are able to both (1) construct a given action as normal and natural, and (2) avoid seeing themselves as personally responsible for said action in any meaningful way.[5]

We see this exact type of paradox when we look at relationships between manhood and violence in American society today. On the one hand, men, like my respondents in the previous chapter, define manhood as predicated on protecting themselves and others from the violence of other men. Put simply, part of their manhood requires them to be ready to dispense violence as a protection against other men.[6] On the other hand, however, they must find a way to naturalize (to make seem natural and normal) men's violence because it is both part of their own identities as men (capable of protecting) and the threat (other men) they use to define themselves as men (protectors).[7] This means they must (1) define violence as a necessary part of being a man, and (2) separate themselves from the men who use violence in "bad" ways. How do they negotiate this paradox?

In this chapter, I examine this question by paying attention to the ways the men I interviewed excuse men's violence. Specifically, they defined violence as a natural element of being a man and an inevitable aspect of society as a whole. In so doing, they repeated stories circulating throughout the nation to explain and excuse why men are violent and, by extension, why they must be ready to be violent themselves at all times.[8] In so doing, they conceptualized men's violence as a necessary part of society that could not be changed, while also distancing themselves from any responsibility for such violence or attempts to change it. These efforts allowed them to accept their own and others' violent manhood while distancing themselves from the bad types of violent men who were the real problem in society.

VOCABULARIES OF MOTIVE

Over the past seven decades, researchers have demonstrated that people create and express a wide variety of explanations for what they consider normal and what they consider abnormal.[9] These explanations are shaped by the social location of the people within a given social context, set of identities, and/or geographic region. Rather than assuming that any given explanation or story about what is right (normal) or wrong (abnormal) is immutable, natural, or automatic, such studies find that our explanations for what we consider to be normal are attempts by people to align their own opinions about what is good with existing social norms defining what is good. They also note that people generally do this whether or not they are conscious of it and whether or not other people might agree with them on any given issue. In fact, this line of scholarship shows that understanding why people think they do anything—no matter how mundane—requires asking how they explain the thing they are doing.

In fact, research in countless areas finds that people mobilize or create "vocabularies" (or ways of communicating) "of motive" (or what they believe) in all aspects of social life. These vocabularies may be used, for example, to explain why racial relations are a certain way, how people choose schools and homes, why a given group can or cannot be legally married, what one should do with their body, how one should treat a given type of person, or what it means to be a good person.[10] They can also aid attempts to lessen social inequalities and attempts to maintain existing societal patterns of racism, classism, sexism, cissexism, monosexism, ageism, and ableism.[11] This is because people can come up with reasons, regardless of intentions, to make anything—no matter how good or bad for themselves or others—appear normal, natural, and necessary to themselves. As a result, anything can become normal, natural, and inevitable through the explanatory attempts of people, but anything can also be rendered abnormal, unnatural, or atypical through the same attempts.

Investigating these patterns in the 1960s, Scott and Lyman[12] outlined how much of social life relies upon the ways people excuse or justify unexpected or untoward phenomena. When something unexpected happens, for example, people create reasons for why and how it happened in relation to the beliefs and norms they already possess. If, for example, a given person believes in a higher power, then that higher power can be used as the reason for anything that happened in their life (e.g., they won the lottery, lost their keys, got or survived cancer, found love).[13] Although this is only one example of this process, it typically plays out in the same manner no matter the people in question. If a given person believes in X (e.g., men should be protectors), then the belief in X can be used as a reason for anything that happens (e.g., that man is aggressive because he is protecting himself from others who might challenge him). This process plays out repeatedly throughout social life as people seek to, consciously or otherwise, create reasons for experiences that make sense in relation to their own beliefs.

Although researchers have expanded on these concepts in various ways over the past few decades,[14] Scott and Lyman pointed out that two of the common elements of this process involve the creation of justifications and excuses. Justifications, they argue, refer to explanations where people accept responsibility for a given phenomenon (e.g., yes I own 75 assault rifles) but deny that said phenomena was inappropriate or abnormal in any way (but there is nothing wrong with owning assault rifles as long as you're a responsible gun owner). In such cases, people admit to doing or saying something deemed abnormal, but then assert that the thing in question was not abnormal or bad in any way. In so doing, they justify their own violation of norms by saying the violation itself is inconsequential. We will return to such justifications in the next chapter, but here we focus on the other most common strategy outlined in the research to date—excuses.

Put simply, excuses are the mirror image of justifications. Specifically, excuses refer to explanations where people accept that X phenomenon is abnormal, inappropriate, or bad (e.g., I realize I have no need for 75 assault rifles) but deny responsibility for any harm that arises from said phenomena (but it's not my fault my child took one of these assault rifles and used it to hurt and/or kill people because they would have just gotten a rifle somewhere else). In such cases, people admit that they did or said something that could have caused harm but then argue that any harm caused was not their fault or at least not *wholly* their fault. This is what the men I interviewed did when presented with the existence of men's violence in society. In such cases, they accepted that men's violence was bad and harmful for society but then argued that it was not their responsibility to change it because it was a normal, natural, and expected part of what it means to be a man.

I focus on these efforts in this chapter. Specifically, I outline the ways the men I interviewed excused men's violence by creating explanations for it that exonerated themselves—and in many cases other men—from any responsibility for such violence. In so doing, they were able to label violence as a problem and also position violent manhood as normal, natural, and not their responsibility to change or oppose in any way. Further, they utilized common narratives circulating in U.S. media and politics to accomplish this explanatory work, which allowed them to excuse violent manhood in ways that potential listeners might empathize and agree with due to the presence of similar explanations in the broader cultural landscape.

MEN'S EXCUSES FOR MEN'S VIOLENCE

It doesn't take training in research to see the epidemic levels of violence in U.S. society today. Whether we talk about mass shootings that appear across our media outlets with such regularity that active shooter drills and other such policies are commonplace in schools, or the rise of #MeToo, Black Lives Matter, and other movements seeking to lessen the violence faced by certain groups within the U.S. population, violence is everywhere. It is also a common component of much of the media we consume, many of the political debates circulating around the nation during and between election cycles, and a common thread of discussion in the realm of international debates and policy concerning potential and existing military conflicts around the world. In fact, this cultural context has led some to suggest that violence itself represents a central element of U.S. national identity in the world. [15]

At the same time, quantitative research regularly finds that people who identify as men are more likely to commit violent acts (and crimes) than other social groups. [16] Researchers also note, like the respondents quoted in chapter 2, that men are often defined in media, scientific, religious, and political domains as people who are supposed to commit violence. [17] Further, researchers demonstrate that the vast majority of gun violence, sexual violence, and domestic violence is typically committed by people who identify as men and often linked to expectations for what it means to be a man in U.S. society, media, and other contexts. [18] Finally, such studies demonstrate that people who identify as men are the ones who are consuming more of the violent media offerings than other gender groups in the United States. [19] The combination of these factors continuously demonstrates deep connections between American culture, definitions of what it means to be a man, and acts and consumption of violence across the nation.

At the same time, however, there is less attention to the ways people who identify as men make sense of such violence and how they make sense of their own positions within society in relation to such violence. Not surprisingly, this was a topic the men I interviewed seemed easily able to discuss and make sense of in their own words. Equally unsurprising, all of them were well aware of the epidemic levels of violence in our society as well as the amount of violent media available to them. Rather than see violence as something to challenge or oppose in any direct way, however, they conceptualized such phenomena as an inevitable force, similar to the old adage of "death and taxes." For them, violence was just something that would naturally occur as a result of, to quote many news programs and my adoptive parents, "boys being boys."

In fact, though likely unintentionally, the men I interviewed echoed prior research on excuses by offering very common explanations for men's violence that did not require them to do anything about such patterns.[20] As a 22-year-old religious respondent I call Damien put it, violence was just part of what it means to be a man:

> Violence is bad, but there is nothing you can do about it. It's just part of being a man. Men are violent. That's it. It's not news or anything complicated. Men are just that way, it's the way we are. The problem is that some men are bad, that's the problem. The bad men are gonna hurt people. It is just gonna happen no matter what you try to do about it.

The conflation of "man" and "violent" was a common refrain for the men I interviewed. As suggested in the previous chapter, it was a built-in component for what they defined as manhood (as opposed to simply a person who might be a man in some other way).

Echoing Scott and Lyman's studies of social norms in the 1960s,[21] biology was one of the main excuses that arose in these conversations. The same way respondents initially said that "male" was what a "man" was before expanding this definition, they would come back to this notion of essential biological manhood when explaining violence in society. These, as Scott and Lyman put it, "appeals to biology" ignore the empirical reality that some men actively work to oppose violence, that many males never identify as men at all, and that assumed biological differences between women and men are often smaller than many people in society believe they are.[22] Derek (22 years old, non-religious) offered a typical illustration of this type of appeal to biology when discussing men's violence in society:

> I think that you have to understand that it's just part of being a guy. You can't let other people disrespect you, so you have to learn to fight. It's not anyone's fault or anything, it's just our nature, I mean, it's just part of being a guy, it's biology or something, learning how to hurt anyone who wants to hurt you, that's just part of it.

Like Derek, many respondents viewed violence as just part of "biology" and "part of being a guy." Nathanial, a 19-year-old non-religious man, put it this way:

> Of course, violence is bad I guess, but for guys, that's just how we're wired. It's part of evolution, we're just naturally built to fight and compete with each other, it's not that anyone wants to be violent, it's just one of those things you can't control because you were born with it.

In fact, this notion of biology as the cause of men's violence also arose in relation to specific types of violence. Talking about domestic violence, for example, Thomas (24 years old, Christian) said: "A lot of the domestic stuff is overblown, men are supposed to take care of the family, sometimes girls today just don't understand that. It's just natural, as a man, to get angry when you're challenged, and I just think girls don't understand that part of how guys are wired." Talking about gun violence, Jim (22 years old, non-religious) added: "Of course guys love guns, we have to, it's part of who we are, it's evolution or something like that. We just like that stuff, we need to be able to know nobody else can make us do something, guns give you that power." In such cases, biology became an explanation for men's violence and suggests that men had no ability or responsibility to change such actions.

As researchers have noted while studying racism, classism, sexism, and other unequal systems throughout the past few decades,[23] biology often provides a powerful excuse for people who seek to avoid responsibility for actions that harm others. This is because, as Scott and Lyman note in their work, "appeals to biology" remove any chance someone has to do something else and transform human actions and decisions into compulsions beyond the control of the humans in question.[24] In fact, this is one of the main reasons that minorities have long been forced to utilize "appeals to biology" to gain civil rights and other legal protections from members of privileged groups.[25] In such cases, the minority group must be protected from the prejudice and discrimination of the dominant group *because* they cannot be expected to conform to the dominant group. In this case, we see the other side of the story: Dominant groups cannot be expected to change oppressive conditions if they can argue they have no ability to change their behavior in ways that could benefit other groups in society.[26]

In fact, this presumed lack of control showed up throughout the interviews. Although biology was the most common excuse the men I interviewed used to suggest that they could not be or expect non-violent forms of manhood, they also utilized what Scott and Lyman refer to as "appeals to intention" and "appeals to accidents"[27] to accomplish the same results. In such cases, respondents—like Mack (22 years old, Catholic) quoted next—defined violence as an unintended consequence of being a man:

> I don't think it's intentional or anything like that. It's just that you have to know how to defend yourself and that means sometimes you have to be violent. It's not that you want to be violent, you just have to sometimes. It's not

like I really want to hurt anyone, but I have to be ready to do whatever I need to do. I think that's really it.

Simon, a 21-year-old Jewish man, added: "I think the problem is that there is violence, yes, but there are also all these things that are unintentional that people want to say is violent when it's really just more like an accident or something like that." Bruce, a 23-year-old non-religious man, added: "Yes, men are violent, but most are good people who don't intend to hurt anyone. Things just happen, you know, and guys just respond without thinking."

These attempts to excuse men's violence via appeals to intention and accidents were most common when the topics of sexual and domestic violence came up in the interviews. The following excerpt from an interview with a 23-year-old Christian man I call Ryan provides a typical case of this type of explanatory work in relation to sexual violence:

> I think it's more of a natural thing, you know, I just don't think it's anything you can control because accidents happen and you didn't mean, or even know, anything bad happened. You just get so hot, and I mean, the girls, they're the ones doing you up like that and getting things going, I mean, you just get excited and things happen because that's just the way it goes, you know, and you can't really help that in the heat of the moment, but then, you know, they misunderstand it, you know, you didn't mean anything, it just happened and then it looks different or something later.

Especially in relation to sexual violence, the men I interviewed were heavily invested in the notion that violence was more often accidental or unintentional. In so doing, they were able to characterize sexual violence as a misunderstanding rather than a problem or a crime.[28] This theme also arose regularly in relation to domestic violence. Domestic violence was generally excused by the men I interviewed because it wasn't "really violence," as the following excerpt from Bryan (19 years old, Christian) illustrates, but rather, an accident or otherwise unintentional thing that "just happens":

> I think domestic issues are usually more of an accident than really violence. I don't think guys mean to be like that because, like, I get it, I sometimes just get so mad and then I may get a little out of control with a girl, but it's not intentional, it's not something I mean to do. It's just that you get angry, and then stuff just happens without you really thinking about it that much. And you don't mean to hurt anyone, not like real violent stuff, you just kind of lose it for a minute.

In such cases, and especially in relation to sexual and domestic violence, the men I interviewed sought to draw a line between (1) real violence that is intentional in some way and (2) accidents that just happen without any real intention. Interestingly, this distinction would make no difference to the person experiencing the violence in question. Violent acts are still violent acts with consequences for the people involved, regardless of intention. As such, this attempt to draw a line between "intentional violence" and "accidental violence" allows the men in question to see violence as something other men do, even if they are (or could see themselves becoming) violent in the same ways as those other men.

At the same time, the men I interviewed also employed another common excuse found throughout research over the last few decades when responding to questions about sexual and domestic violence: scapegoating. Scapegoating refers to attempts to blame something external for the actions or statements of a given person. Put simply, it is the effort to suggest something else (i.e., the scapegoat) is the problem rather than the person or people involved. As illustrated by the following excerpt from a 20-year-old non-religious man I call Scott, the media was the scapegoat my interviewees preferred when excusing sexual and domestic violence:

> Okay, this might sound bad, but with the rape thing, I think that is something the media did. I mean, girls get all these ideas about how it's supposed to be, and then when it's not what they expected, that's when they start saying something was wrong. But I think in most cases it's just something they come up with because they got this idea from the media and the real thing wasn't like that so they think it's just worse than it is.

Echoing this sentiment when talking about domestic violence, a 24-year-old religious man I call Marty offered the following explanation:

> I feel like domestic violence is one that the media has completely blown out of proportion. I don't mean that in a bad way. I just mean that couples fight, it happens, it's not a big deal. Okay, yeah, sometimes you might take it too far and shove her or something, but's not that serious, guys are just kind of aggressive and girls know that. But then when girls don't get their way, then shit gets crazy, and it's just usually some made-up stuff she said and the media just jumping on it so they can get attention.

Especially considering that even cases where sexual and domestic violence are officially reported suggest these are serious and regularly occurring social problems and that research demonstrates that many (or even most) of this violence doesn't even get reported,[29] my respondents' attempts to explain away such topics mirror many discussions of mainstream violence.[30]

Although I return to these topics in more depth in later chapters, the ways the men I interviewed excused sexual and domestic violence offer insights into public debates about these topics. When media outlets cover charges and accusations against, for example, the president, movie executives, movie stars, judges, and other high-profile men, the men who view these reports may be ready to dismiss them because they already view these issues as media events rather than real, serious violence in society. In the same way, these excuses speak to why so many media pundits spend time discussing the possible intentions or plans of a given man who is accused of violence. This may be because the men I interviewed distinguish between what they consider real intentional violence and accidental unintentional acts that may have a violent component. Taken together, the ways men excuse existing patterns of violence in society suggest that any attempts to combat violence will necessarily require finding ways to overcome or dismantle such explanatory efforts.

In fact, this observation may be even more important when we recognize that one of the main ways the media and politicians often talk about men's violence actually aligns with the excuses provided by the men I interviewed. Whether talking about intentions, potential scapegoats, biology, or accidents, for example, an overarching theme in the ways they excuse violence in society involves drawing a line between normal activities and men on the one hand, and actually violent activities and men on the other hand. As illustrated by the next quote from a 20-year-old non-religious man I call Caleb, they often do this the same way our media and politicians do it, by suggesting the real problems are psychological or mental:

> I don't really think violence is as much of a problem as it seems. I mean, a lot of these debates and movements are just unnecessary. Think about it, it's how men are wired, it's a mental thing we have. Sometimes, that wiring goes wrong and then you have crazy people who just go violent in bad ways, but most men are just going to use violence the way we should use it, you know, protection, just like our brains are made to do.

A non-religious 23-year-old man I call Lenny had a similar take: "Violence is one thing, but the problem isn't violence, it's psychological. It's when people take things too far because they don't understand how to act, that's the issue." A 24-year-old atheist I call James added: "I'm a psychology major, and I can tell you, men are just made violent. It's in our brains, but the bad stuff happens when something goes wrong in the brain and you can't stop that."

These explanations mirror media cycles discussing "mental illness" and "brain chemistry" each time examples of mass violence occur in society. As other researchers have noted, however, such explanatory frameworks rely on the assumption that violent men are exceptional rather than a common case of behavior among men and limit discussion of men's violence to individual examples rather than examining common occurrences in such patterns over time.[31] Further, these types of explanations ignore the empirical reality that the vast majority of mentally divergent people are not violent in any special way and that the assumption that all men's brains are wired for violence is also an assumption without proof. Rather than discussing violence itself, these types of frameworks utilized by the media and by my respondents provide excuses for violent manhood that separate "men's violence" from "men" by arguing that it is only the rare, unusual man who would commit such acts in the first place.

In these ways, the men I interviewed mobilized excuses for men's violence in society that allowed them to continue to argue that violence is part of being a man, but that only the "bad men" (i.e., not them) were likely to do what they considered real or problematic violence. This rhetorical conceptualization of violent manhood as natural but other men's violence as problematic allowed them to navigate the paradox wherein violence is defined as bad, but manhood is defined as something (good) that relies on violence. Thus, they symbolically positioned themselves as the "good men" who might unintentionally harm people and defined others as the "bad men" who committed what they identified as real, intentional violence against others. In so doing, however, they reinforced the notion that men are supposed to be violent and avoided any responsibility they might have, as men, to combat either their own or other men's violence.

FROM EXCUSES TO JUSTIFICATIONS

Overall, the men I interviewed made sense of violence by mobilizing excuses for agreeing that violence in society was a problem but removing themselves from any responsibility for combatting such violence. They did this by symbolically drawing a line between the "bad men" who intentionally commit violence and themselves and other "good men" who might be violent in some way as simply a part of being a man. Whether they drew on biology, accidents, intentions, psychology, or scapegoating to manage this explanatory work, the real problem was consistently *other* men who did not properly control their essential manly violence (rather than the interconnectedness of violence and manhood itself). As such, their efforts allowed them to maintain the belief that violence is simply *a* part of manhood while also distancing themselves from the consequences and responsibility for violence enacted as part of *other* men's performance of manhood.

As suggested earlier in this chapter, excuses like the ones my interviewees mobilized to make sense of violence in society are often utilized in combination with justifications wherein people take responsibility for doing abnormal or potentially bad things but then deny that their activities are in any way problematic. In the next chapter, I examine how the men I interviewed shifted to this type of explanatory effort when faced with questions about guns, gun violence, and mass shootings in society. Whereas the idea of violence itself led them to distinguish between themselves and those who are really violent, the idea of guns led them to shift explanatory strategies to maintain their conceptualization of violence as a part of manhood *and* men's violence as a problem that other men were responsible for in society.

NOTES

1. Grace and Ozzi, *Tranny*; Mock, *Redefining Realness*; Sumerau, *Cigarettes & Wine*; Sumerau, *Homecoming Queens*; Sumerau, *Palmetto Rose*; Sumerau and Cragun, *Christianity and the Limits of Minority*; Sumerau and Mathers, *America through Transgender Eyes.*
   2. If readers are unfamiliar with these instances, they can google the names Donald Trump, Roger Ailes, Brett Kavanaugh, Bill Cosby, Kevin Spacey, Harvey Weinstein, Brock Turner, Bill O'Reilly, Johnny Depp, Louis C.K., and Matt Lauer, just to name a few.
   3. Goffman, "The Arrangement between the Sexes"; Goffman, *Interaction Ritual*; Goffman, *Presentation of Self in Everyday Life*; Goffman, *Stigma*; Mills, "Situated Actions and Vocabularies of Motive."
   4. Scott and Lyman, "Accounts."
   5. See also McCabe and Sumerau, "Reproductive Vocabularies," and Sumerau, "Some of Us Are Good."
   6. Ezzell, "Pornography, Lad Mags, Video Games, and Boys"; Garland, Branch, and Grimes, "Blurring the Lines"; Kelley and Gruenewald, "Accomplishing Masculinity"; Lageson, McElrath, and Palmer, "Gendered Public Support"; Messerschmidt, "Becoming 'Real Men'"; Mullaney, "Telling It Like a Man"; Ravn, "I Would Never Start a Fight"; Scully and Marolla, "Convicted Rapists' Vocabulary"; Sweet, "The Sociology of Gaslighting"; Taylor and Jasinski, "Femicide and the Feminist Perspective."
   7. Martin, "Gender, Accounts, and Rape Processing Work"; Martin, *Rape Work*; Schrock and Schwalbe, "Men, Masculinity, and Manhood Acts"; and the references in note 6.
   8. Connell, *Gender and Power*; Messner, *Guys Like Me*; Metzl, *Dying of Whiteness.*
   9. Doering, "Face, Accounts, and Schemes"; Martin, "Gender, Accounts, and Rape Processing"; Mathers, "Bathrooms, Boundaries, and Emotional Burdens"; McCabe and Sumerau, "Reproductive Vocabularies"; Mills, "Situated Actions"; Silva, "Public Accounts"; Sumerau, "Some of Us Are Good."
   10. Bonilla-Silva, *Racism without Racists*; Fetner, *How the Religious Right*; Heath, *One Marriage under God*; Rohlinger, *Abortion Politics.*
   11. Martin, *Rape Work*; Park, "Choosing Childlessness"; Samuels, *Fantasies of Identification*; Scherrer, Kazyak, and Schmitz, "Getting 'Bi' in the Family"; Sumerau, "Some of Us"; Sumerau and Mathers, *America through Transgender Eyes.*
   12. Scott and Lyman, "Accounts."
   13. Cragun and Sumerau, "God May Save Your Life."
   14. Doering, "Face, Accounts, and Schemes"; Mathers, "Bathrooms, Boundaries"; McCabe and Sumerau, "Reproductive Vocabularies"; Silva, "Public Accounts"; Sumerau, "Some of Us."
   15. Collins, *Black Sexual Politics*; Messner, *Guys Like Me*; Sumerau and Mathers, *America through Transgender Eyes.*
   16. Becker and McCorkel, "The Gender of Criminal Opportunity"; Boyle, "Social Psychological Processes"; Carlson, "Mourning Mayberry"; Huff-Corzine, McCutcheon, Corzine, Jarvis, Tetzlaff-Bemiller, Weller, and Landon, "Shooting for Accuracy"; Steffensmeier, Zhong, Ackerman, Schwartz, and Agha, "Gender Gap Trends for Violent Crimes."
   17. Schrock and Schwalbe, "Men, Masculinity, and Manhood Acts."
   18. Boyle and Walker, "Neutralization and Denial of Sexual Violence"; Garland, Branch, and Grimes, "Blurring the Lines"; Garland, Policastro, Branch, and Henderson, "Bruised and Battered"; Moloney and Love, "Assessing Online Misogyny."

19. Branch, Hilinski-Rosick, Johnson, and Solano, "Revenge Porn Victimization of College Students"; Ezzell, "Pornography, Lad Mags"; Lageson, McElrath, and Palmer, "Gendered Public Support"; Moloney and Love, "Assessing Online Misogyny."

20. Sumerau, Forbes, Grollman, and Mathers, "Constructing Allyship."

21. Scott and Lyman, "Accounts"; see also Goffman, "The Arrangement"; Goffman, *Interaction Ritual*; Goffman, *Presentation of Self*; Goffman, *Stigma*.

22. Davis, *Contesting Intersex*, Karkazis, *Fixing Sex*; Samuels, *Fantasies of Identification*; Stryker, *Transgender History*; Sumerau and Mathers, *America through Transgender Eyes*.

23. Collins, *Black Feminist Thought*; Smith, *The Everyday World as Problematic.*

24. Scott and Lyman, "Accounts."

25. Duggan, *The Twilight of Equality?*; Ferguson, *Aberrations in Black*; Stone, "The Empire Strikes Back."

26. Bonilla-Silva, *Racism without Racists*; Collins, *Black Feminist Thought*; Schwalbe, Godwin, Holden, Schrock, Thompson, and Wolkomir, "Generic Processes in the Reproduction of Inequality."

27. Scott and Lyman, "Accounts."

28. Martin, *Rape Work*; Venema, Lorenz, and Sweda, "Unfounded, Cleared, or Cleared by Exceptional Means."

29. See the sources in note 28.

30. See also Sweet, "Sociology of Gaslighting."

31. Bergstrand and Jasper, "Villains, Victims, and Heroes"; Canan, Jozkowski, Wiersma-Mosley, Blunt-Vinti, and Bradley, "Validation of the Sexual Experience Survey"; Venema, Lorenz, and Sweda, "Unfounded, Cleared."

Chapter Four

Arming Manhood

One of the first times I realized that guns meant something very different in academic settings than in the working-class Southern spaces where I grew up arose near the end of my second year after finishing graduate school. A colleague at a private university asked me, "Why don't you ever seem as stressed as the rest of us?" in a joking manner.[1] I responded in a similarly joking manner: "Well, once you've had a gun in your face, there isn't really anything about research and class deadlines that can get to you all that much." My colleague's face turned white and he began to stutter and stammer in search of a response. I had to calm him down by making a couple other jokes to ease—unexpected for me—the tension that had arisen just because my colleague was standing beside someone who did not see guns or violence as only theoretical issues or research problems to think about or study.[2]

I thought about this moment in passing as my phone exploded with messages of concern—and fear—from colleagues and friends the morning after the Pulse Massacre in Orlando, Florida, in 2016.[3] I was in north Florida at the time, far away from the violence that fell on the bar that night, but some of my colleagues knew I sometimes went to that bar and others in the Orlando and Tampa Bay areas. At the same time, for some of my colleagues, I'm one of the few or the only LGB and/or T person they regularly interact with in their daily lives, and this point seemed to become more relevant to them in the aftermath of the attack.[4] Like so many others that morning, I was grieving while also feeling grateful that I was, at least for the moment, somewhat safe from the worst aspects of violence against LGBT people in the United States at present.[5] I thought about these things as I made my way back to the Tampa Bay area from north Florida as best I could and much as I had regularly for years at that point.

The following year I was once again thinking about how violence does or does not touch a given person's life in a real, visceral way when news broke of a serial killer active in Tampa.[6] I watched as colleagues and students with little direct experience with violence reacted in shock, disbelief, and fear that I somewhat recalled from the first few times I experienced violence in a more direct way in my life.[7] A colleague who had been at least somewhat friendly and spoke at length about his confusion that I didn't feel safe in the United States when he took such safety as a given, for example, increasingly became more and more tense and combative with others after becoming aware and afraid of an active serial killer nearby. As I was one of the only people in his life intimately familiar with violence at the time, and a person to whom he had expressed his deep belief in safety at times in the past, social psychologists would not be surprised that I became one of the people he found intimidating as he managed his newly realized lack of safety, fear of violence, and potential for an unexpected death (i.e., the loss of his prior beliefs).[8]

Each of these examples speak to an important aspect of violence studies—the difference between violence in the abstract and violence as lived, visceral experience.[9] When one is privileged or lucky enough to believe violence is an abstract thing that they are safe from (e.g., I am safe, it won't happen to me), said person is much more likely to be able to, as the men I interviewed did in the last chapter, find ways to explain it that remove themselves from the phenomenon or any responsibility for it. On the other hand, however, once one encounters violence as a real, concrete part of their own lives (e.g., it could happen to me), they are likely to seek some way to compensate for (1) losing their belief of being safe from violence by (2) trying to re-establish a sense of control that might allow them to *feel* safe again.

In fact, previous research demonstrates that people who identify as men are likely to engage in such strategies of compensation whenever they feel their sense of control challenged or otherwise threatened in any way.[10] Since the central element of the varied forms of contemporary manhood that researchers have identified concerns the ability to both exert control over others and avoid being or feeling controlled by others, any situation where men feel like they have lost control (e.g., of their finances, safety, sexuality, bodies, careers, or families) can become a situation where they feel the need to engage in what scholars call "compensatory manhood acts" or emphasizing and/or exaggerating elements of ideal manhood to re-establish their feelings of control and thus their possession of manhood.[11] In such cases, men respond to perceived slights, violations of their beliefs about the world, or other unexpected events by seeking to re-establish a sense of control in another area of their life.

Historically, compensatory manhood acts may take a wide variety of forms. A man who feels he has lost a truth he held dear (e.g., belief in God, safety, an essential purpose for life, or some other supernatural claim), for example, may seek to fortify other truths he holds dear (e.g., people should do this health behavior, people should agree with this statistic, people should be part of this religion, people should live this way).[12] In other cases, a man who feels he has lost control of his body (via illness, injury, or even an elective medical procedure) may seek to re-assert the use of his body (e.g., by driving while medicated despite the risk, or purchasing and showing off a certain type of vehicle or other technology deemed impressive by others).[13] In such cases, the perceived loss of control in one element of the man's life overflows into a desire to utilize another element of his life to compensate for the perceived loss.

Throughout history, violence represents one of the most common strategies for men to compensate for perceived slights, insults, or other situations where they feel they have lost control. In some cases, this takes the form of structural violence wherein a man utilizes his higher standing in a structure to attack someone else's career, economic security, or other standing to demonstrate to himself that he can control the outcomes of others.[14] In other cases, this takes the form of interpersonal violence wherein a man utilizes his connection to another person (e.g., a spouse, a child, a friend) to exert control over said person's life through displays of anger, the threat or act of physical and sexual violence, and/or emotional manipulation.[15] In all such cases, the man in question engages in violence to impact and/or control others as a way of compensating for feeling out of control in some area of his life.

As noted in chapter 1, my central argument throughout this book is that men's violent actions represent compensatory manhood acts any man may engage in when they feel out of control in some way. Although researchers typically focus on the ways men who are marginalized via racism, classism, heterosexism, ageism, and other factors compensate for such marginalization,[16] here I utilize the experiences of men who occupy privileged positions in terms of race, class, sexuality, and age to demonstrate that such strategies are an element of manhood itself rather than simply a strategy adopted by marginalized men. To this end, the last two chapters outlined the ways the men I interviewed defined violence as an essential part of manhood and excused the continued presence of violence in society. In this chapter, I demonstrate how the combination of these beliefs (i.e., violence is part of manhood and may be excused as such) allows violence to exist as a potential compensatory manhood act for any man at any time when he feels the need to compensate for a perceived lack of control in his own life, regardless of what other privileges he may possess at the time.

To this end, I utilize the case of gun violence to demonstrate how the men I interviewed conceptualize guns as a metaphor for the ability to take back control when they feel insecure, unsafe, or otherwise out of control.[17] In so doing, I demonstrate how their own desire to have a way to compensate for negative events translates into justifications for gun violence and possession, predicated upon their belief that manhood requires violence and that violence is excusable in some circumstances. I also demonstrate how each of the most commonly cited reasons for mass shootings and other gun violence mirror ways men report feeling a loss of control (in relation to ideal manhood) in their own lives.[18] In so doing, this chapter demonstrates how violence can be seen as a compensatory manhood act predicated upon both definitions of what it means to be a man and the ways men excuse other men's violence.

VIOLENCE AS A COMPENSATORY MANHOOD ACT

Although researchers have almost entirely conceptualized compensatory manhood acts as strategies men occupying subordinated race, class, sexual, and age identities practice to define themselves as real men, they all find that men, regardless of demographics, engage in such strategies as a result of feeling out of control in their lives. However, such studies rarely consider that, since life is full of situations where one cannot control some or all elements, all men will feel out of control at some time in their lives and thus potentially seek to compensate for these feelings. This presents a question for existing studies of compensatory manhood acts because such studies generally show how men in marginalized populations compensate by adopting and presenting the behaviors, codes of conduct, and other norms of men in dominant racial, classed, sexual, and aged populations.[19] If men are already able to pass or be seen as members of the dominant population or the ideal man, how do they compensate when they feel out of control in one or many ways throughout their own lives?

I argue the answer to this question is violence. Whether such violence is enacted or merely threatened, for example, it involves taking control over someone else, at least temporarily. Whether such violence is emotional, physical, sexual, structural, or a combination of these types, it involves exercising control over others in some way. Even if such violence is done by men to themselves, it demonstrates to said men that they have control over themselves even if they do not possess control over other things. Maybe even more importantly, violence is an act of control (over self or others) with immediate—often visible—results, which may be especially effective in forestalling a given man's sense of being out of control. Finally, violence provides an opportunity for men to demonstrate control to themselves and others in a way that is already defined as part of being a man. Thus, men are already armed with excuses for such acts throughout the existing social context wherein such violence may occur.

This line of thinking also finds voice in some of the work on compensatory manhood acts among marginalized populations of men.[20] Examining the compensatory manhood acts of racial minority men, for example, researchers have shown that a common strategy includes the ability to appear and/or demonstrate toughness and power through fighting, violent criminal activity, and/or the destruction of property.[21] Similar findings can be seen in examinations of compensatory manhood acts among lower- and working-class men of various racial identities.[22] In fact, often the violent strategies of compensation in such groups are basically the same. Further, even research into the compensatory manhood acts of gay, bi, and trans men suggests violence, or at least the threat of violence in structural, emotional, sexual, and physical forms, may be utilized by such men to demonstrate that they are really men.[23] Put simply, even men in marginalized groups who may adopt elements of the hegemonic ideal predicated on racial, sexual, classed, and other norms may turn to violence as a form of compensation in many cases.

As I outlined in chapters 2 and 3, these patterns are not surprising when we consider that violence is often defined as an essential aspect of manhood. If, for example, manhood is defined as, at least in part, the ability to engage in violence (whether, as my respondents put it, to protect self and others or otherwise), then it is not surprising that people can demonstrate they are really men to themselves and others by engaging in violence. At the same time, if men's violence is something that even men who do not consider themselves violent work to excuse and explain as normal and inevitable, then such explanatory work opens the door for any man to engage in violence and then draw on existing excuses to explain why it was not necessarily a bad or unexpected thing for them to do so. This means that whether or not men use it at any points in their lives, violence is always a tool that men can use to demonstrate to themselves and others that they are, in fact, really and truly men.

With these things in mind, we can look at the reasons men often feel out of control or less than "real" men to see situations where men are likely to engage in violence. If, for example, cultural notions of manhood define men as economic providers for themselves, their families, and others, then it is not surprising when men who lose their jobs, do not accomplish what they consider enough economically, or otherwise feel economically average or less than average engage in violence against themselves[24] (alcohol, drugs, fight clubs, suicide, etc.) or others (domestic abuse, rape, mass shootings, fights, harassment of women and other minorities, etc.) to re-establish a sense of themselves as real men. Although this is just one example, we can hypothesize similar pathways whenever men are not, as cultural narratives say they should be, more successful than women and other gender populations, sexually desirable, strong, powerful, tough, leaders, virile, popular with other men, right and rational in their thinking, or in line with any other elements of ideal manhood in any given society. In each case, violence provides a type of safety valve (e.g., something any man can do) to re-establish their vision of themselves as "real men" who exercise control and avoid being controlled by others.

As such, I utilize the following sections to illustrate this type of pathway between feeling out of control (not a man) and responding to such feelings with violence (seeking to show one is a man) via the case of gun violence. I use this case because (1) it is currently a very serious social problem in the United States that garners significant media attention and political discussion, (2) it is a type of violence overwhelmingly committed by people who identify as men,[25] and (3) it is an area of scholarship where researchers, mostly in criminology, have long outlined the most common reasons for its occurrence. In fact, when we combine insights from studies of men with studies concerning the stated reasons for gun violence,[26] it becomes clear that each of the common reasons for gun violence outlined in criminological studies are also common reasons why people who identify as men engage in compensatory manhood acts in many contexts and cases.

THE VOCABULARIES OF MOTIVE FOR GUN VIOLENCE

As noted in chapter 3, people regularly establish "vocabularies of motive," or explanations, for why they do or say a given thing in a given social context. Although the actual motivations that may lie behind a given statement or action are beyond the scope of existing scientific methods due to the complex bio-psycho-social processes occurring in any given brain at any given time, the ways people explain why they think they did a given thing give researchers an opportunity to examine what conscious reasons people believe led to their actions.[27] As a result, a common element of research over the past 80 years involves ascertaining what people *say* motivates a given set of behaviors, and every major social problem provides opportunities wherein researchers seek to garner such information.

As is the case with other social problems, gun violence in the United States is something many researchers have sought to understand.[28] Whether we look to high-profile mass shootings occurring with regularity in schools, shopping centers, and other public places, or less visible examples of assaults, murders, and other gun violence occurring each day in our nation, gun violence is a topic that has garnered more and more attention in recent years. Part of this attention involves the use of surveys, interview studies, experiments, and ethnography to ascertain why people say they do or do not engage in gun possession, gun violence itself, attempts to limit gun access, attempts to expand gun access, activism related to gun control policies, and a wealth of other questions related to the presence of guns, gun violence, and debates about these two things throughout the United States today.[29]

In so doing, criminologists have noted that a similar list of explanations is often provided for any type of gun violence, from mass shootings to individual crimes, and that these explanations have held fairly steady for at least the last three or four decades. Specifically, researchers have outlined five common elements in the stated motivations for gun violence throughout the past half-century. Research in this area terms these five elements as (1) revenge, (2) power, (3) loyalty, (4) terror, and (5) profit.[30] Revenge refers to gun violence meant to pay back someone or something that has made the shooter feel like a failure in some way. Power refers to gun violence meant to demonstrate control over others. Loyalty refers to gun violence meant to spare someone from misery or other negative outcomes. Terror refers to gun violence meant to send a message to others who do not appear to respect or value the shooter in question. Profit refers to gun violence meant to acquire economic resources that the shooter believes they cannot realistically acquire another way. As criminologists have shown, almost all gun violence can be explained, by scholars and others, as the result of someone experiencing one of these common elements—or a combination of them—in their own life.

Considering that the vast majority of gun violence is committed by people who identify as men,[31] it is surprising that such insights have not really found voice in connection with studies of what it currently means to be a man in the United States. Considering that men are supposed to be successful in economic, familial, and other fields, for example, it would make sense that gun violence based on revenge might be a common compensatory strategy available—regardless of use—for many men. We can make the same connections throughout the five common elements. Considering that the hallmark of manhood is to be in control and not be controlled, for example, the power explanation for gun violence can be understood as saying gun violence itself is just an exaggerated or more extreme manhood act. Likewise, considering that men are supposed to protect themselves and others from harm, the loyalty explanation for gun violence may be men compensating for a perceived failure as protector by ending the perceived pain of others and their own perceived failure to protect others via a gun. Further, since men are supposed to be respected, the terror explanation may be a compensatory strategy for reestablishing respect when men feel it has been taken away in some manner. Finally, since men are supposed to be economically successful and the breadwinners for families, the profit motive could be an extension of this element of manhood (if I can't provide in other ways, I can use a gun to get the things to provide for myself and my family).

As table 4.1 demonstrates, whether we call these "explanations for gun violence" (as criminologists do) or "reasons for compensatory manhood acts" (as gender scholars do), we may be talking about multiple versions of the exact same social process without realizing it due to the lack of integration of gender and masculinity studies, on the one hand, and criminological studies of violence, on the other. In fact, I admit that even with my own experience of violence during my life, gender studies training, and criminological training, I never made the connection until I interviewed these respondents and asked about their thoughts on gun violence, as well as manhood and violence more broadly. In my interviews, however, the men I spoke with made clear the connections between the two as they sought to both (1) denounce gun violence in the abstract while also (2) justifying the possession of guns and gun violence itself as understandable aspects of being a man in contemporary U.S. society.

Table 4.1. Reasons for Gun Violence or Compensatory Manhood Acts?

Explanation of Gun Violence	*Compensatory Manhood Act*
Revenge	Reaction to perceived failure as a man
Power	Reaction to feeling out of control
Loyalty	Reaction to inability to protect others
Terror	Reaction to perceived slight or disrespect
Profit	Reaction to inability to provide for others

COMPENSATORY MANHOOD ACTS AND THE JUSTIFICATION FOR GUN VIOLENCE

As I noted in chapter 3, justifications are explanations for a given act or for accepting responsibility for the act (e.g., I own a handgun), but then argue that the act is acceptable and not necessarily bad or wrong in any way (e.g., but I'm a responsible gun owner who would never use it for ill purposes). In such cases, the person admits that the act or belief is problematic (e.g., I know I should have done better on the test), but then argues that their own behavior—or that of others—is understandable or acceptable (e.g., but that test was just too hard). Rather than seeking to explain how the act or belief wasn't potentially harmful or bad, as is the case with excuses (see chapter 3), justifications explain that even if the belief or act was potentially bad, it was acceptable or at least understandable for some reason. In this section, I demonstrate how the men I interviewed utilized this type of explanatory work when discussing gun violence and the ways these efforts leave in place the possibility of themselves or others committing such violence as a bad—though understandable, in their eyes—compensatory manhood act.

It is important to note that all the men I interviewed agreed that gun violence was a serious problem and that the possession and accessibility of guns was a big part of the problem. A typical illustration of this shared belief came from a 22-year-old Christian I call Mark:

> I don't think anyone can ignore that gun violence is a serious issue. I mean, look at the news and it seems like it's worse than ever with all the shootings and stuff. I mean, there seem to be crazy people carrying guns into every school and movie theater, it's insane and it just has to stop, simple as that.

For Mark and the other men I interviewed, there was no question about either the levels or the morality of gun violence in the U.S. today. Echoing many others, a 22-year-old non-religious man I call Derek added: "Shootings are just out of control man, that stuff is scary as hell, little kids can't even go to school without worry about being shot, what kind of insanity is that?" Whether religious or non-religious, the men I interviewed agreed that gun violence was a bad thing and that it was something that needed to be addressed in the United States today.

Importantly, these statements differ from the ones in chapter 3 concerning violence in society more broadly. Whereas the men I interviewed found ways to excuse violence as a general phenomenon by defining it as not necessarily a bad or unexpected thing for men to engage in under certain circumstances, gun violence was seen as definitely a bad thing that needed to be addressed. Unlike their responses regarding sexual and domestic violence, the respondents' statements did not suggest the media was creating or otherwise exaggerating gun violence. Rather, the observation of media coverage concerning gun violence, and mass shootings especially, was, as a 22-year-old agnostic I call Jonathan put it, "Showing us just how bad it is, every day, on television and social media, it's just everywhere, and you can't see that and not realize it's a real problem."

What do we make of this difference? When the media emphasizes concerns about sexual and domestic violence—or violence more broadly in the society—in its coverage, then the men I interviewed conceptualize this coverage as overblown. If, on the other hand, the same media shows mass shootings and other gun violence with regularity, then the men I interviewed see such reports as evidence that gun violence is a serious issue. Although this seems to be an obvious contradiction on the part of the men I interviewed, it can also be seen as an example of the ways that violence is perceived when it is or is not directly associated with men themselves. For example, most coverage of domestic and sexual violence focuses on men's violence against women, while coverage of gun violence focuses on men's violence against everyone. In the first case, my respondents are able to mobilize excuses for forms of violence that are less likely to impact them in a direct manner (at least as far as they are concerned or media coverage suggests). In the second case, however, they are faced with violence that is more likely to impact them personally and thus this type of violence is seen as a serious issue and problem that must be resolved.

In fact, this distinction became even more clear when I asked the men I interviewed how they felt about potentially facing violence in their own lives. In most cases, as illustrated by the following excerpt from a 22-year-old religious man I call Damien, they differentiated between what they were and were not afraid of in terms of violence:

> It's a different thing if we're talking about rape and things like that because it's hard to tell what is or is not, you know, but when you're talking about guns and school shootings and that kind of thing, well then, yeah, of course I worry about that because that is pretty cut-and-dried and could happen anywhere. You know, I don't think about stuff like gangs or missiles or any of that either, you know, but guns are different because they're everywhere; you don't have to be in the army or some kind of war zone for that.

A 19-year-old non-religious man I call Lucas added: "I think the difference is that I can understand somebody with a gun, I get that, that's just a pissed-off dude, so that one is more of a real threat than other stuff." Gun violence was more serious, and more real, to the men I interviewed because they could see it happening to them, and as a result, they had trouble distancing themselves from it the same way they did with other types of violence.

It would be nice to assume that an awareness of the ways gun violence could impact their own lives would lead the men I interviewed to favor efforts to decrease such violence. However, this was almost entirely not the case. Rather, 45 of the 50 men I interviewed were not in favor of gun control policies, social movement groups seeking to promote political and policy action on gun violence, or efforts to limit or regulate gun possession and acquisition in the United States. Even the five who were in favor of such measures when asked in a direct manner suggested at other times in the interview that such efforts would be ineffective because, as one put it, "Guns will always be available and people will just find other ways to get them." As such, the men I interviewed admitted concerns about gun violence, agreed that gun violence was a serious problem that needed to be solved, but also did not support efforts to combat this problem. As the quote above from Lucas suggests, this was because the men I interviewed saw gun violence as something they could at least understand, even if they didn't think they would ever do it themselves.

The idea that gun violence was something the men I interviewed could understand brings us back to the integration of criminological and gender studies outlined in the previous section. Although the men I interviewed could have followed their admission that gun violence was a serious problem with a commitment to seeking remedies for the problem, they instead followed the pathway of justification[32] by explaining why gun violence, as well as men's possession of guns, was *actually* understandable and to be expected. To do this, they drew on similar patterns outlined in the studies of compensatory manhood acts I referenced in the previous section to explain the ways men might compensate for various perceived slights by owning and using guns. In fact, it seemed like the men I interviewed were well versed in both the common reasons for committing gun violence noted in existing research[33] and the ways these reasons mirror elements of ideal manhood.

The typical progression of these types of justifications involved first arguing that gun violence was a terrible problem and then explaining that, even so, it was something that could make sense in some ways. Trevor, a 23-year-old Christian man, offered a typical illustration of this process when discussing gun violence:

> The world has just gone crazy, people are shooting each other left and right at schools and everywhere else, and that is terrifying; something needs to be done about it. I think the problem, though, is that people don't try to understand it, and so what are you going to do about it? Nothing probably, I mean, like think about the guys that do this stuff, I mean, on the news, they're like, not doing well in their jobs or they've lost their kids or that kind of thing, I mean, I get it, they just couldn't do what they're supposed to do so they snapped, you know, they went crazy because they just couldn't deal with having a bad job or I don't know, whatever failure they were going through.

Like Trevor, the men I interviewed recognized that gun violence was a problem, but they also came up with reasons why men would engage in such acts. In so doing, they regularly suggested that failing to do the things a man is supposed to do could transform men into "crazy" shooters who "snapped" and enacted violence upon others.

They also regularly argued that guns were an important part of life as a man and that negotiating gun violence, in some cases, was just part of being a man in the United States today. Adrian, a non-religious 22-year-old, for example, stated: "Sometimes I wonder what people expect, I mean yeah, normal people aren't planning armed robberies, but if you have no other way to provide for your family, what are you supposed to do?" A 21-year-old Jewish man I call Micah added: "Look, I'll just tell you that many guys have guns because that is a way to make sure nobody messes with you, and the problem is just that people take that too far sometimes." A 20-year-old atheist I call Roger also noted: "Nobody is taking my gun or my dad's guns, it's just not happening, we just use them for hunting, but it's also a guy thing, you know, a sign of respect and power." Echoing many others, a 23-year-old Christian I call Ryan stated: "You don't own guns to use them, but you own them in case you have to use them. You have to be ready to defend yourself and that's just the way the world is nowadays." In each case, the possession and potential to use guns serves as a symbolic marker of manhood and an understandable element of men's lives in relation to existing social norms and expectations.

These cases also demonstrate the usefulness of conceptualizing common reasons for gun violence as forms of compensatory manhood acts. Whether we consider Micah's justification for a man utilizing violence in the name of profit and providing for others, or Roger's conceptualization of guns as a source of power and respect in comparison to shooters who commit gun crimes to feel powerful and establish respect, the seeds of potential gun violence exist within the ways the men I interviewed make sense of gun possession itself. Whether a man has guns "to defend" himself or to "make sure nobody messes with you," the ingredients for potential gun violence exist in the reasons these men give for wanting or possessing guns themselves before any concrete violence occurs. In fact, these statements beg the question: Would these respondents commit gun violence if they felt a certain level of disrespect, powerlessness, or loss of control at some point in their lives?

The two answers to this hypothetical question are maybe and maybe not. In the latter case, maybe they would find other ways to compensate for moments where they felt their manhood threatened in some way, or even move away from ideal notions of manhood to find healthier ways of accepting the inevitable moments when any human feels out of control. In the former case, however, maybe they would utilize guns to compensate for moments where they felt their manhood threatened, or maybe they would do so if their manhood were threatened a certain amount over time. The problem, of course, is that there is no way to predict which of these answers might become reality in the case of any given man within a nation that defines violence as part of manhood. Since any man can justify the possession or use of guns by labeling it both a problem and in some ways understandable, the rest of society can only wait to see which ones will—or will not—utilize guns or other instruments of violence to engage in compensatory manhood acts.

In fact, this exact dilemma became even more clear when the men I interviewed directly explained why gun violence, of varied types, was at least understandable from their perspectives. For example, a 22-year-old non-religious man I call Jim stated: "It worries me, but I can kind of understand the shooters sometimes. I mean, many of them seem to feel so alone and like they are not man enough, and I've felt that way before, and I worry about that." Striking a similar chord in the midst of his assertion that all men need to have guns, a 24-year-old Christian man I call Thomas added: "I try to not judge too much because I have guns, I know how to use them, and I don't know what I would do if, like, I lost my family or had no job or something like that, I mean, I don't think I would hurt anyone like that, but what if I'm wrong about that." In such cases, the men I interviewed wrestled with the realization that, in some ways, they could relate to men who had engaged in gun violence, and especially mass shootings, even though they wanted to believe that they could never do the same.

These observations demonstrate two important things about the relationship between manhood and violence in contemporary U.S. society. First, even men capable of theoretically reaching the hegemonic ideal of manhood will feel the need to compensate in situations and settings where they feel their manhood is challenged in one way or another. Second, the same men, even if they have no documented violent history to date, may be able to recognize themselves and empathize with other men who engage in gun violence or other types of violent behavior. As I argue throughout this book, the combination of these insights suggests that understanding relationships between violence and manhood requires deconstructing and transforming what it means to be a man in the minds of men themselves.

RELATIONSHIPS BETWEEN VIOLENCE AND COMPENSATORY MANHOOD ACTS

In this chapter, I utilized the case of men's interpretations of gun violence to outline how violence itself may be a kind of compensatory manhood act. Specifically, I argue that men who feel marginalized in any way—no matter how temporarily—may respond to such marginalization by engaging in violence to reclaim their sense of themselves as real men. To illustrate this point, I utilized the case of gun violence and the ways the men I interviewed both (1) defined gun violence as a problem and, at the same time, (2) conceptualized it as an understandable and expected element of manhood. In so doing, I outlined the ways that criminological insights concerning why people engage in gun violence mirror gender studies' insights into why people engage in compensatory manhood acts. I also demonstrated how the men I interviewed suggest that any man can—and maybe should—accept potential violence as part of being a real man in contemporary U.S. society.

Although gun violence offers an illustrative example of the ways violence and compensatory manhood acts intertwine in the lives of men, this pathway is not limited to gun violence or any other specific form of violent behavior. Therefore, I utilize the next chapter to outline the ways that violence as a compensatory manhood act may be witnessed in men's descriptions of sexual and romantic relationships with women. Specifically, I outline how the men I interviewed define sexual relationships in violent terms and conceptualize such relationships in terms of power and control. In so doing, I outline how the same pathway demonstrated in the case of gun violence (i.e., that men may find such violence understandable as a reaction to feeling out of control or less manly) finds voice in their negotiation of relationships, domestic and sexual violence, and perceptions of non-heterosexual others.

NOTES

1. Sumerau, *Cigarettes & Wine*; Sumerau, "Embodying Nonexistence"; Sumerau, *Homecoming Queens*; Sumerau, "I See Monsters"; Sumerau and Mathers, *America through Transgender Eyes*.

2. This was my original interpretation of his reaction, but it was also later confirmed in another conversation with the same colleague.

3. For discussion of the Pulse massacre, see Acosta, "Pulse: A Space for Resilience"; Lampe, Huff-Corzine, and Corzine, "The Pulse Scrolls"; and Sumerau and Mathers, *America through Transgender Eyes*.

4. As is common in universities today, I am one of the few openly LGBT faculty members at my university.

5. James, Herman, Rankin, Keisling, Mottet, and Anafi, *Report of the 2015 U.S. Transgender Survey*; Movement Advancement Project, "A Closer Look"; Schrock, Sumerau, and Ueno, "Sexualities"; Steele, Collier, and Sumerau, "Lesbian, Gay, and Bisexual Contact."

6. See Figueroa, "Accused Seminole Heights Killer."

7. I was also afraid, though I was not shocked and had long been aware there was plenty of violence in Tampa and other parts of Florida.

8. Hale, "Fear of Crime"; Tudor, "A (Macro) Sociology of Fear?"; Wiest, *Creating Cultural Monsters*.

9. Branch and Richards, "The Effects of Receiving a Rape Disclosure"; Jauk, "Gender Violence Revisited"; Kallivayalil, "Narratives of Suffering"; Martin, *Rape Work*; Richards and Branch, "Relationship between Social Support and Adolescent Dating Violence."

10. Cheng, "Marginalized Masculinities"; Eastman and Schrock, "Southern Rock Musicians"; Ezzell, "I'm in Control"; Schrock and Schwalbe, "Men, Masculinity, and Manhood Acts"; Snow and Anderson, "Identity Work among the Homeless"; Sumerau, "That's What a Man."

11. Schrock and Schwalbe, "Men, Masculinity, and Manhood Acts"; Sumerau, "That's What a Man."

12. Schrock and Schwalbe, "Men, Masculinity, and Manhood Acts"; Sumerau, Padavic, and Schrock, "Little Girls Unwilling to Do."

13. Courtenay, "Constructions of Masculinity"; Cragun and Sumerau, "Losing Manhood Like a Man"; Vaccaro, "Male Bodies in Manhood Acts."

14. Ridgeway, *Framed by Gender*; Roscigno, Garcia, and Bobbitt-Zeher, "Social Closure and Processes of Race/Sex Employment Discrimination."

15. Kallivayalil, "Narratives of Suffering"; Schrock, McCabe, and Vaccaro, "Narrative Manhood Acts"; Schrock and Padavic, "Negotiating Hegemonic Masculinity"; Sweet, "Sociology of Gaslighting."

16. For examples, see note 10.

17. Carlson, *Citizen-Protectors*; Carlson, "Legally Armed but Presumed Dangerous"; Dowd-Arrow, Hill, and Burdette, "Gun Ownership and Fear."

18. Berg, "Trends in the Lethality of American Violence"; Huff-Corzine, McCutcheon, Corzine, Jarvis, Tetzlaff-Bemiller, Weller, and Landon, "Shooting for Accuracy"; Phillips and Maume, "Have Gun Will Shoot?"

19. See the citations in note 10.

20. Again, see the citations in note 10.

21. Anderson, *Code of the Street*; Cheng, "Marginalized Masculinities"; Ferguson, *Bad Boys*.

22. Eastman and Schrock, "Southern Rock Musicians"; MacLeod, *Ain't No Makin' It*; Snow and Anderson, "Identity Work."

23. Schilt, "Just One of the Guys?"; Sumerau, "That's What a Man."

24. Ezzell, "I'm in Control"; Schrock and Padavic, "Negotiating Hegemonic Masculinity."

25. Berg, "Trends"; Huff-Corzine et al., "Shooting for Accuracy"; Phillips and Maume, "Have Gun Will Shoot?"

26. Messerschmidt, *Masculinities and Crime*.

27. Mills, "Situated Actions"; Scott and Lyman, "Accounts."

28. Berg, "Trends"; Carlson, *Citizen-Protectors*; Carlson, "Revisiting the Weberian Presumption"; Dowd-Arrow, Hill, and Burdette, "Gun Ownership"; Hill, Dowd-Arrow, Davis, and Burdette, "Happiness Is a Warm Gun?"; Huff-Corzine et al., "Shooting for Accuracy"; Phillips and Maume, "Have Gun Will Shoot?"

29. For examples, see Fox and DeLateur, "Mass Shootings in America"; Fox and Levin, "Multiple Homicide"; and Schleimer, Kravitz-Wirtz, Pallin, Charbonneau, Buggs, and Wintemute, "Firearm Ownership in California."

30. Fox and DeLateur, "Mass Shootings"; Fox and Levin, "Multiple Homicide."

31. Huff-Corzine et al., "Shooting for Accuracy."

32. Scott and Lyman, "Accounts."

33. See citations in note 29 for examples.

Chapter Five

Sexual Manhood

I've been teaching college classes on sexualities for almost a decade as I compose this book.[1] In such classes, we read and talk about things like consensual sexual activity, practices and strategies for pleasurable and healthy sexual behaviors, social and cultural variation in sexual norms and expectations, and the variety of sexual identities, attractions, and identifications. In some ways, each of these courses is different because the group of students in the class will demonstrate more interest and desire for one aspect of a given sexual topic or another. In other ways, these classes share similarities as students in general seek to understand ways to create healthy relationships, increasingly visible LGBT communities in society, and the frequency and other elements of sexual violence in the United States today. The classes also all have another thing in common: very few people who identify as cisgender heterosexual men are ever in them.[2]

I was thinking about these observations in 2016 when I made the difficult choice to write an essay about the first time I was raped, which I allowed friends to use in their classes.[3] I remembered realizing that sexual violence would be a common topic of sexualities courses the first time I offered any lessons or classes on the topic in graduate school. I remembered how that forced me to face the sexual violence I had experienced in ways that took a lot of work (still ongoing) to be more comfortable with over time. I remembered and re-experienced the shame and fear that I tried so hard to run away from until that point. I thought about all these things as the essay went from my fingertips to the hands of others, and even more so when I decided to publish it as a chapter in an edited volume my spouse and I were working on at the time.[4]

As I've shared with more than a few friends and family members, I also think about the composition of that personal essay as the spark that ignited my writing and publishing of sociology-based novels about lesbian, gay, bisexual, and transgender (LGBT) experience in the U.S. South.[5] Although I did not intend for it to happen, I am not completely surprised that sexual violence comes up in discussion each of the many times that I have been talking about these books with students in one or another college classroom across the country. I am also not surprised when readers express both gratitude and distaste (sometimes from the same person) for examples and discussions of the violence LGBT people and cisgender heterosexual women face within my novels. In such cases, readers echo students and others I interact with throughout my life who navigate sexual violence—on some level and in some way—as they negotiate daily life.

Each of these examples speak to the relevance of sexual violence in the United States today. Whether we talk about the abuse of children, street harassment, rape and sexual assault of varied types, hate crimes and structural violence against LGBT people, domestic violence of varied types, or the election of a president who boasted about various types of sexual violence during his campaign,[6] the specter of sexual violence looms large throughout the nation. At the same time, however, news cycles seem to provide a never-ending series of cases wherein people accused of or even caught in the process of sexual violence suffer little to no negative outcomes as a result. Further, social media and other internet arenas continuously fill with repeated examples of harassment, sexual threats, violent pornography, and stories celebrating and defending people who commit sexual violence.

The combination of these and other elements of contemporary U.S. society have led some scholars to refer to our nation as a "rape culture,"[7] or a culture in which sexual violence is defined and treated as normal and natural. In fact, one only needs to view U.S. news and political pundits each time a new high-profile case of sexual violence enters the airwaves to hear commentators talk about harassment and rape as normal things boys just do and as natural elements of male bodies and brains created by some evolutionary mechanism that is never specified in any real detail. As researchers have noted over the past few decades, the high levels of sexual violence in the United States are not remotely surprising within such a context.[8] Rather, such a context encourages sexual violence through the ongoing creation of narratives, symbols, and other representations defining sexual violence as something that will likely occur no matter what anyone else does, says, or otherwise attempts to the contrary.

Importantly, this is exactly what the men I interviewed suggested when they talked about sexualities and sexual violence itself. Specifically, they defined sexuality itself in violent terms predicated on exercising control over themselves and others and drew on these definitions to downplay concerns about sexual and other types of violence expressed by women and sexual minorities. In this chapter, I explore these conceptualizations to illustrate that, as in the case of meanings related to guns, men may arm themselves with sexual meanings that allow the possibility of utilizing violence as a compensatory manhood act. In so doing, I demonstrate how constructions of sexual manhood predicated on violent heterosexism allow the men I interviewed to define sexual violence as a normal and natural element of social life.

THE CREATION OF HETEROSEXUALITY

Rather than an immutable or natural phenomenon, historians demonstrate that heterosexuality is a concept that was created over time in relation to existing political and social forces.[9] Although there are entire works on this topic, for our purposes, heterosexuality refers to a sexual identity wherein one develops or identifies a preference for sexual and/or romantic contact only for people with different sex and/or gender identifications. At the same time, heterosexuality, like manhood and other social identities, is something people individually and collectively construct over time and in relation to their other deeply held beliefs, traditions, and meaning systems.[10] In this section, I examine how the men I interviewed define heterosexuality.

To this end, it is important to note that the men I interviewed were responding to a simple prompt about heterosexuality itself. The same way I began our discussions by asking them "What does it mean to be a man?" I asked them later in the interview, "What does heterosexual mean?" to initiate the discussion on sexuality and issues related to sexual violence in society. I took this approach, with these and other questions, for two reasons. First, I did not want to assume what it means to be heterosexual to these men or to anyone else in the course of the interview.[11] Rather, I was interested in what the term meant to each of them specifically because definitions of sexual terms can vary dramatically between individuals. Second, as I did with definitions of manhood discussed in chapter 2 and of whiteness discussed in the next chapter, I sought to allow the men I interviewed to define what it means to be a man in racial, gendered, sexual, and other terms themselves for the purpose of this analysis. As such, I sought to learn their own constructions of manhood rather than assume an existing type. Here I share what the men I interviewed did to create heterosexuality as a meaning in their own lives.

Echoing their definitions of what it means to be a man, the men I interviewed defined violence as an essential part of heterosexuality. I do not mean to suggest they intended to do this in any conscious way. Rather, the ways they chose to talk about the subject regularly involved the implication of violence. One way they did this involved referring to sexual acts themselves via violent metaphors whereby they sought to, for example, "bang," "break," "hurt," "nail," "destroy," "conquer," "beat up," and/or "annihilate"[12] pussy, women, girls, asses, and other recipients of these violent terms. As scholars have noted in other studies,[13] this type of rhetoric both (1) suggests the other person or people one has sex with is an object to be harmed in some way, and (2) equates collective sexual interactions (two or more people pleasing each other sexually) with violent interaction (two or more people harming each other through violence). As such, this type of wording implies the dehumanization—consciously or otherwise—of sexual partners and the transformation of other people into receptacles for violent acts.

The other way heterosexuality as a violent act emerged in their definitions involved conceptualizing heterosexual activity as a conquest of another human being. Jacob, a 22-year-old Christian, offered a typical example of this type of statement:

> Part of being a guy is just being aggressive in sexual stuff, it's like a game or a fight or something, she is going to do the thing they do, you know, play hard to get, and it's up to you to just push past that and get in there. That's just the kind of game we play, girls and guys I mean, they try to slow you down and you try to push through that to get where you need to be. It's kind of like sports, you gotta get through there to score, that's the fun part.

As if reading from the same playbook in an American football game, many of the men I interviewed used sports analogies to conceptualize heterosexual activity as an attempt to conquer or otherwise overcome another person. For example, a 20-year-old non-religious man I call Darryl shared: "Heterosexuality? I guess it's the game, you know, the way you try to score, and the girl tries to make it hard to score, I guess that's it."

It is telling that the men I interviewed expected resistance to sexual advances. Rather than something people would mutually agree on as a result of shared desire (e.g., a way heterosexuality or any other sexual identity could be defined by people), they typically framed heterosexual activity as a competition of winners and losers wherein one would get what they wanted and the other would, at best, concede defeat of a sort. As a 23-year-old religious man I call Craig put it, heterosexuality was a sexual contest that men expected to win:

> Look, girls are just different, but they get the way it works. My last girlfriend is a good example, she didn't want sex as much as I did, but she would give it to me sometimes even when she didn't really want it because that's what a good woman does. She understood that, and I had respect for her because of that, because I knew she knew how to take care of a man. Not all girls get it though, but that's how it is, men, we just want more, that's it, it's how we are.

For Craig and others, sexual activity, as well as their conceptions of themselves as heterosexual men, relied on the construction of men as conquerors who "want more" and women as those who should be conquered to satisfy such wants.

Rather than an exception to the rule, violence was a common ingredient in the ways the men I interviewed defined their own sexuality. As implied in this section and expanded on in the next section, this conceptualization of heterosexuality as a violent act created the conditions for seeing sexual violence as, at best, just a form of heterosexual activity. Whether they were defining sexual acts as violent things they wanted to do to women or sexual activity itself as a competition where they would win no matter what defenses women might develop, this interpretive work defined sexual activity itself through the lens of violence. As such, much like the influence of their definitions of manhood on their reaction to other forms of violence, their own definitions of heterosexuality created conditions for their reactions to sexual violence.

VIOLENT CISGENDER HETEROSEXUAL MANHOOD

After ascertaining the ways the men I interviewed defined heterosexuality itself, our interviews shifted into a discussion about sexual violence in society. In so doing, I asked them for their opinions on rape, sexual harassment, violence against LGBT people, violence against women, and domestic violence. In the following section, I outline their responses in relation to existing research concerning violence against cisgender heterosexual women and LGBT populations. Further, I discuss how their responses illustrate their own conceptualization of what others would call sexual violence as what they would see as reactions to men experiencing a loss or perceived loss of control (what scholars would call compensatory manhood acts, as discussed in detail in chapters 1 and 4).

Violence against Women

In its simplest terms, sexism refers to prejudice and discrimination on the basis of sex and gender. Existing scholarship is littered with examples of men's sexism against women of various types in workplaces, schools, politics, sports, families, religious organizations of various types, relationships, public spaces of all types, cultural arenas like music and the arts more broadly, and police forces.[14] In fact, it is harder *not* to think of places where researchers have found empirical patterns of men's sexism against women at this point in history, and research consistently demonstrates that such patterns emerge and maintain themselves as a result of negative beliefs and opinions men internalize about womanhood and anything labeled feminine throughout their lives. This has led scholars to conceptualize the sexism women and other feminine people face as one of the fundamental and foundational aspects of contemporary social organization in the United States.

In fact, violence against women is often conceptualized as a direct result and creator of sexism in society.[15] When examining violence against women, for example, researchers continuously find that men's negative attitudes toward women provide fuel for the establishment, threat, enactment, and/or justification of such violent acts. Further, researchers consistently demonstrate how violence reinforces sexist beliefs about the supposed power of men and assumed weakness of women in the social world. Moreover, researchers have demonstrated that even the threat of violence that women navigate throughout their lives can have dramatic effects upon their biological health and emotional experience of the life course. It is thus not in any way surprising that the correlation of heterosexuality and violence implied by the men I interviewed found voice in their reactions to violence against women in society.

As illustrated in chapter 3, the men I interviewed often engaged in victim-blaming and other forms of denial to excuse violence against women. Talking about domestic violence, for example, the men I interviewed argued that the issue was not as serious as the media suggests, as illustrated in this quote from a 24-year-old Christian I call Thomas: "It's all just women getting angry, couples fight, it happens, they just blow it out of proportion and the media goes along with it." Lenny, a 23-year-old non-religious man, added: "I don't know if that's a real thing. Feminism has these women thinking all kinds of stuff, but really, men are in charge in the relationship and that's just the way it's supposed to be." Although some might expect this type of thinking to be the norm only among the religious men,[16] non-religious men—like a 19-year-old I call Evan—would beg to differ: "Domestic violence, if you can call it that, is more of a media thing than a real thing." Scott, a 20-year-old non-religious man, added: "I don't have anything to say on the domestic crap because I'm not sure if that's even a real thing."

Of course, when I followed up initial questions (e.g., "What do you think about domestic violence?") with another question (e.g., "Why do you feel that way?"), it was not surprising that the reasons given always relied on sexist stereotypes painting women as overly emotional or otherwise untrustworthy. A 21-year-old atheist I call Lewis offered a typical example:

> I just think it's more of a misunderstanding that happens because women get emotional about some kind of fight or something. I don't think it's really violence they're talking about, but more like they didn't get their way and now they're mad and they know saying something about it can make the guy look bad. I think that's kind of it, they just get upset and don't know how to control their feelings, it's that kind of thing.

A 20-year-old religious man offered a similar explanation: "Relationships are tough, you're gonna fight, and sometimes that means the woman will get all emotional and make something out of nothing." Although I would assume it was unintentional, the men I interviewed thus echoed the statements of convicted batterers by utilizing stereotypical depictions of emotional women to excuse or otherwise dismiss concerns about domestic violence.[17]

The same kind of dismissal came up repeatedly related to domestic violence, rape, and sexual harassment. In the latter case, the men I interviewed were especially concerned with what they considered "imaginary" sexual harassment. A 21-year-old Christian man I call Lee, for example, had this to say about harassment: "I think the problem is women have forgotten how to take a compliment, and that might not be their fault even, but it's just a made-up kind of imaginary thing, guys are just saying you look hot, that's not a bad thing, just ask the ugly girls." Echoing this sentiment, a 20-year-old agnostic I call Edward said: "There is no such thing as harassment, we talked about this in one of my classes, it's just some PC[18] type stuff where girls can't take a compliment anymore, that's all it is." Of course, many women have shared stories about harassment over the years, and one of the cardinal aspects of such cases is that unwanted commentary on one's body can feel threatening instead of complimentary. This is especially true because, as noted in the last chapter in relation to guns, there is no way for women to know in advance which man will or will not follow unwanted commentary on their bodies with other forms of unwanted attention.[19]

Although the above examples demonstrate men's dismissal of common types of violence against women, they also demonstrate the importance of maintaining control in the minds of these men. When dismissing domestic violence, for example, the men regularly conceptualize such activities as situations where things "got out of control," and the reports of women (speaking out about domestic violence in some way) as attempts by these women to gain control (i.e., get their way). Likewise, they reject the idea of harassment by suggesting they should have control over (get to decide) whether women want to experience men's attempts to interact or engage with them, which allows them to suggest reports of harassment come only from women who resist such control. This notion that violence against women, whether harassment or domestic in nature, represents a negotiation of control (i.e., men attempting to exercise control against women who don't want it) brings us back to the central thesis of this book: violence as a way men compensate for any situation where they are not or feel they are not in enough control over others.

This theme within the data became even more explicit when the subject of rape arose in the conversations. Specifically, this occurred in two primary ways when the men I interviewed responded to the topic of rape. First, they often defined rape, like domestic violence and harassment, as an overblown issue. Thomas, a 24-year-old Christian, offered a typical example:

> Well, I think a lot of the things people call rape aren't really rape. Things can get out of control in the bedroom or wherever, and as a guy, you just get so wound up. I don't think that's a rape, sometimes girls just get shy or change their mind or something and you can't do anything about that in the moment, so I think that's more of like a misunderstanding than anything else. I mean, sure, there are like criminals and real rapists out there, but most of the stuff people talk about is just some girl changing her mind or something and that's not really rape I don't think.

Here, Thomas dismisses rape accusations by reframing them as misunderstandings while also suggesting that control is important to the situation (e.g., the guy can't control himself and the girl tries to do so by changing her mind), but he also hits the second main way my respondents talked about rape: they suggested that real rape was somewhere "out there," done by "someone else," and disconnected from them and their experiences.

These two ways of talking about rape emerged throughout the interviews. Rape was a misunderstanding when it was in a situation that they could imagine themselves in (e.g., drinking, a partner changing her mind about sex) whether they had been or not, but it was "real rape" when it was somewhere else in an abstract situation disconnected from their own lives. Roger, a 20-year-old atheist, offered another illustrative example:

> Well, first, what do you mean by rape, I mean, some people think if a girl has too much to drink or something that it's rape, and that's just silly; she just regretted the sex. That is not the guy's fault, probably not hers either. She just changed her mind, it happens, fine, but that's not really rape. But rape is a thing, I mean, you can look at the news and TV and stuff like that, there are some crazy dudes out there that will beat up girls and rape them and all kinds of stuff, and that's a serious problem that we need to do something about, so I guess you have to be clear about what kind of rape, like what one person says is rape or like real bad rapes that you hear about 'cause those are not the same.

Again, as evidenced in their conceptualizations of themselves as violent protectors against "the real violent men" in chapter 2, the men I interviewed sought to distinguish between things they might do that are considered rape by others and things they would not do, which also constitute rape. In so doing, they maintained the notion that heterosexual activity is a contest (e.g., they should push past any resistance up to a point) but drew the line at some abstract notion of behaviors other men would engage in, behaviors that they considered the real violence.

As recent criminological and sociological studies have noted, these observations suggest that men separate themselves from questions about men's and other violence against women.[20] Specifically, they see personal situations where they could imagine themselves as one of the participants, different and distinct from abstract situations where other, unknown men interact with women. In so doing, they draw lines between their own activities that might be seen as violent by women and opponents of violence against women and the actions of imaginary "other men" that they agree are examples of violence against women. Whether intentional or otherwise, these types of mental gymnastics allow them to express opposition to violence against women even if they are acting in ways that would be considered by others to be violence against women. As a result, they dismiss the role of their own notions of normal heterosexual manhood in the experiences of violence women face, report, fear, and otherwise navigate in U.S. society.

Violence against LGBT People

Similar to research on sexism, scholarship has long demonstrated recurring societal patterns of heterosexism, monosexism, and cissexism throughout contemporary U.S. society.[21] In the first case, researchers demonstrate how non-heterosexual people are discriminated against, individually and as a group, in every major social institutional sphere. Similarly, in the second case, research reveals how social authorities from families to government to religious institutions to the media promote and enforce monosexism (i.e., the belief that one must only be either hetero- or homosexual in activity, identity, and inclination) throughout society. Finally, in the third case, researchers have shown how even perceptions of the natural and supernatural worlds that U.S. residents inhabit are based on the assumption of two and only two sexes and genders and how such patterns provide the initial discrimination necessary for sexism in society.

Not surprisingly, violence is a mechanism whereby such patterns are maintained throughout society.[22] Whether we look at hate crimes targeting lesbian and gay couples or trans women (especially trans women of color), we see violence as a way to enforce notions of heterosexism and cissexism in society. If we look at the high levels of inequalities bisexual and transgender people continue to face in relation to medical access, housing, and economic opportunities, we see structural violence that renders much of these populations subject to negative health, economic, and violent outcomes across the nation. Likewise, when we view the continuing difficulties lesbian women face with sexual harassment in public spaces or gay men face in athletic venues, at least the threat of violence remains a very real part of much of the LGBT experience in the United States, despite many gains in social recognition for this population over the last half century. As I have noted elsewhere,[23] there is not a single aspect of contemporary interactional or structural U.S. society where patterns of hetero-, mono-, and/or cissexism cannot be witnessed in some form.

Although I wasn't sure what to expect from the men I interviewed when the subject of violence against lesbian, bisexual, and transgender women arose, previous research suggested it would be similar to and yet different from their responses about "women" as an abstract category (that they might interpret as cisgender or heterosexual only). In fact, such research was correct, and many of the same things were said about transgender, bisexual, and lesbian women—as well as concerns about rape, domestic violence, and harassment—as were said about women as a whole when I asked without any modifier or adjective. At the same time, there were differences that were specific to each group. Specifically, the men I interviewed saw lesbian women, as more than one put it, as "kind of strange, but more like competition than real women." A 19-year-old Christian I call Adam offered the most common response in this regard: "Lesbians are kind of a different thing, they're okay I guess. I mean, I know a few, but they're not like real women, they're more like guys who are more fun to look at." Harry, a 21-year-old atheist, added: "Lesbians are fun man, it's like another guy, and they only get annoying when they try to be like girls."

Though the men I interviewed downplayed or simply dismissed the womanhood of lesbian women, they emphasized the sexual womanhood of bisexual, pansexual, fluid, and queer women. A 24-year-old Catholic I call Erving shared a common response in this regard:

> The bi girls are just, well, I don't mean to sound mean or judgmental, but they're just figuring things out, they're finding themselves, and so I feel like once they get the right guy they will kind of settle down and act like women are supposed to. I think the bi thing doesn't really exist in the same way; it's more like a kind of phase where they're trying to find something that they feel like they're missing and so it's not like a permanent thing.

As is often the case in U.S. society, Erving defines womanhood as ultimately mono- and heterosexual. Sexually fluid women, as a 23-year-old non-religious man I call Dwayne put it, are expected to ultimately become "just like any other [heterosexual] girl; they just need to find the right guy, and once they do, that's the end of all the pretend lesbian stuff." Caleb, a 20-year-old non-religious man, added: "Look, lesbians are born that way, but the pan ones or whatever they call themselves are just confused, they're gonna meet a good dude and figure it out." In such cases, the same womanhood these men dismissed regarding lesbian women became heterosexual potential emphasized in the case of bi+ women.

This distinction between lesbian and bi+ women seemed to become mixed together in the case of transgender women. Specifically, transgender women were seen as very sexual (like bi+ women) and, at the same time, not really women either (like lesbian women). Echoing narratives from conservative political movements, trans women were seen as, for example, "intimidating," "dangerous," "aggressively sexual," "gay men in dresses," and "tricking people." The following excerpt from a 19-year-old non-religious man I call Nathanial offers a typical example:

> I don't know what to say about the transgenders, they are just insane, I think. I mean, they get up all sexual and stuff with makeup and whatever else they use, but then they're really just dudes, you know, they're just trying to make you think they're a woman, and that's messed up because, I mean, I'm not gay but some of them are so good with that stuff that they trick you and you think they're hot, but then it's like no, they're just these intimidating things, I mean, not things, I guess, I mean, they're just scary dudes and you might not know that at first.

As suggested by Nathanial's comments, trans women were "intimidating" or otherwise problematic because they could attract men who both (1) considered themselves to be heterosexual while (2) only considering cisgender women to be women. The possibility of being attracted to non-cisgender women (even though that would still be considered heterosexual attraction according to many people throughout society because trans women are women regardless of what their current sex status is or may ever be)[24] led the men I interviewed to conceptualize trans women as a looming threat.

Much like the narratives historically promoted by conservative religious social movements,[25] this same type of logic could be seen in the men's responses to gay men. However, likely due to rising social acceptance of gay men in U.S. society in recent years, they conceptualized gay men as both a potential threat and a potential friend at the same time. Mason, a 19-year-old non-religious man, offered a typical example: "Look, I have gay friends so I'm not homophobic or anything, but I think gay guys can get in trouble because some of them take it too far with flirting and stuff, and I'm not saying that makes it okay, but guys aren't gonna just put up with that." Allen, a 23-year-old religious man, added: "I like gay people and some of the guys are pretty cool, but some of them, I don't know man, they get so in your face with it, you know, and I think that's probably what happens in situations where they get hurt." Echoing a similar pattern to what scholars call colorblind racism, the men I interviewed suggested they were okay with gay people (e.g., I'm not homophobic, but . . .), but that *some* gay men were problematic and potentially at fault for violence they experienced at the hands of other men who might feel their heterosexuality threatened by the existence of these gay men.

However, this type of interpretive work became more complicated in the case of bisexual, pansexual, queer, and transgender men. In such cases, the men I interviewed argued that these groups did not really exist. Rather, they saw bi+ men as "confused" or "really just gay guys who are figuring things out," and trans men as "women who kind of get confused" in most cases. As a 24-year-old atheist I call James put it: "Gay and lesbian people are okay, and sure girls can go through phases and transgenders can put on a dress, but I don't think a guy can be born a girl or like boys and girls, not a real guy at least, I just think that takes things too far." Rather than a threat or a potential friend, bi+ and trans men were seen as a supernatural or otherwise imaginary thing that the men I interviewed did not accept as real or credible in their version of the world. In so doing, they denied fluidity—of gender or sexuality—was even possible for "real" men.

At the same time, there were two more groups I asked about that the men I interviewed were fairly certain didn't really exist at all: non-binary people and asexual men. In the former case, the men I interviewed rarely said anything about the population, even when asked, other than to say non-binary gender identities were not a real thing and not something they had even come across in their own lives, outside of media, to their knowledge. In the case of asexual men, their disbelief was even more explicit, and often followed with comments like the following quote from a 22-year-old Christian man I call Mark: "But then that's not a man, men are naturally built to be sexual, we can't help it, there is no way to be a guy and not want sex." Similar to the possibility of bisexual and transgender men whose existence would violate their own assumptions of sexual manhood predicated upon heterosexual, cisgender status, non-binary people and asexual men were dismissed as not even a possible part of these men's understanding of the world.

Asexual women, however, garnered a different reaction from the men I interviewed. Rather than nonexistent, asexual women were seen as a potential, as many of the men put it, "obstacle" or "problem" they expected to encounter. This was not because they were more open-minded in terms of accepting asexual women, but rather because they generally argued, as a 22-year-old non-religious man I call Zack put it, "Well yeah, any girl might say she doesn't like or want sex, but that's just part of the game they play, the guy has to chase and they play hard to get, but that's just the way it works, it's not that they really don't want it." Blending their dismissal of common types of violence against women with their conceptualization of heterosexual manhood as a game of conquest, the men I interviewed saw asexuality among women as just one more form of defense that men were supposed to navigate.

MANHOOD IN MOTION

Throughout this chapter I shared the ways the men I interviewed made sense of sexual violence in society in relation to their own conceptualizations of heterosexuality and manhood. Rather than just a sexual preference, they defined heterosexuality itself as an expression of violence aligned with their notions of men as (at least potentially) violent beings. In so doing, they were able to conceptualize violence against cisgender heterosexual women, asexual people, and LGBT people more broadly in two separate ways. First, there were things they could see themselves doing that they defined as not really violence. Then there were things that really are violent that they assumed other people did to women or that sexual and gender minorities did something to provoke. In all such cases, they maintained notions of manhood as predicated on control and violence as a compensatory strategy for responding to situations wherein men were not in control of themselves or others.

The examples in this chapter also bring us back to an element in respondents' original definitions of what it means to be a man: protection. Specifically, their separation of what counts and does not count as real violence offers protection for themselves from concerns that they might be the bad types of violent men. At the same time, their utilization of victim-blaming techniques suggests that they feel the need to always protect themselves from potential challenges. In the next chapter, I expand on these observations by discussing the ways the men I interviewed made sense of movements seeking to challenge men, men's violence, and men's privilege in the wider social world. In so doing, I demonstrate how they conceptualize such movements as attacks on manhood itself and seek to protect their existing definitions of manhood as predicated on at least the potential for violence.

NOTES

1. Simula, Sumerau, and Miller, *Expanding the Rainbow.*
2. For example, the class I'm teaching as I finish writing and revising this book includes one cisgender heterosexual man, and like many of the others who have taken the class, he is a member of another marginalized group (i.e., an immigrant in this case).
3. Sumerau, "I See Monsters."
4. Nowakowski and Sumerau, *Negotiating the Emotional Challenges.*
5. Sumerau, "Some of Us Are Good"; Sumerau, "Somewhere between Evangelical and Queer"; Sumerau, "That's What a Man"; Sumerau, Cragun, and Mathers, "I Found God"; Sumerau, Padavic, and Schrock, "Little Girls Unwilling."
6. Hlavka, "Normalizing Sexual Violence"; Holland and Bedera, "Call for Help Immediately"; Jauk, "Gender Violence Revisited"; Mathers, "Bathrooms, Boundaries"; Pascoe, "Who Is a Real Man?"; Relman, "The 25 Women Who Have Accused Trump"; Scaptura and Boyle, "Masculinity Threat, 'Incel' Traits, and Violent Fantasies"; Sweet, "The Sociology of Gaslighting."
7. Bedera and Nordmeyer, "An Inherently Masculine Practice"; Ezzell, "Pornography, Lad Mags"; Friedman and Valenti, *Yes Means Yes!*; Garland, Branch, and Grimes, "Blurring the Lines"; Hollander and Pascoe, "Comment on Brush and Miller's 'Trouble in Paradigm.'"
8. Ezzell, "Pornography, Lad Mags"; Gossett and Byrne, "Click Here"; Hlavka, "Normalizing Sexual Violence"; RAINN, "About Sexual Assault"; Robinson, "Violence Against Women"; Scaptura and Boyle, "Masculinity Threat."

9. Boag, *Same-Sex Affairs*; Foucault, *History of Sexuality*; Katz, *The Invention of Heterosexuality*; Schrock, Sumerau, and Ueno, "Sexualities"; Ward, *Not Gay*; Warner, *The Trouble with Normal*.

10. Abelson, *Men in Place*; Barber, "Men Wanted"; Butler, *Gender Trouble*; Garcia, *Respect Yourself*; Hamilton, "Trading on Heterosexuality"; Mathers, Sumerau, and Ueno, "This Isn't Just Another Gay Group"; Pascoe, *Dude, You're a Fag*; Rich, "Compulsory Heterosexuality"; Rogers, *Trans Men in the South*.

11. As with manhood, one could say this is especially important as I do not identify in this way myself and might therefore lack understanding of how people who claim the identity make sense of it.

12. These quoted words each refer to statements multiple men made using the same terms.

13. Friedman and Valenti, *Yes Means Yes*; Martin, *Rape Work*.

14. Acker, "Inequality Regimes"; Collins, *Black Feminist Thought*; Lubold, "Breastfeeding and Employment"; Martin, "Said and Done"; Serano, *Whipping Girl*; Smith, *The Everyday World as Problematic*; Sumerau, Padavic, and Schrock, "Little Girls Unwilling"; Thorne, *Gender Play*.

15. Connell, *Gender and Power*; Martin, "Gender as a Social Institution"; Martin, *Rape Work*; Messerschmidt, *Masculinities and Crime*.

16. Avishai, "'Doing Religion' in a Secular World"; Barringer, Gay, and Lynxwiler, "Gender, Religiosity, Spirituality"; Burke, *Christians under Covers*; Moon, *God, Sex, and Politics*; Sumerau, Mathers, and Cragun, "Incorporating Transgender Experience."

17. Ezzell, "I'm in Control"; Schrock and Padavic, "Negotiating Hegemonic Masculinity."

18. PC is shorthand for "politically correct."

19. Sweet, "The Sociology of Gaslighting."

20. Pascoe and Hollander, "Good Guys Don't Rape"; Richards, Branch, and Ray, "The Impact of Parental and Peer Social Support"; Sweet, "The Sociology of Gaslighting."

21. Eisner, *Bi*; Mathers, "Bi+ People's Experiences"; Schilt and Westbrook, "Doing Gender, Doing Heteronormativity"; Serano, *Whipping Girl*; Sumerau, Cragun, and Mathers, "Contemporary Religion"; Sumerau and Grollman, "Obscuring Oppression."

22. Bedera and Nordmeyer, "Never Go Out Alone"; Bridges, "A Very 'Gay' Straight?"; Bridges and Pascoe, "Hybrid Masculinities"; Crenshaw, "Mapping the Margins"; Jauk, "Gendered Violence Revisited"; Pascoe and Diefendorf, "No Homo"; Spade, *Normal Life*; Steele, Everett, and Hughes, "Influence of Perceived Femininity, Masculinity"; Sumerau and Mathers, *America through Transgender Eyes*; Walters, Chen, and Breiding, *National Intimate Partner and Sexual Violence Survey*.

23. Schrock, Sumerau, and Ueno, "Sexualities"; Sumerau and Cragun, *Christianity and the Limits of Minority Acceptance*; Sumerau and Mathers, *America through Transgender Eyes*.

24. Bellwether, *Fucking Trans Women*.

25. Fetner, *How the Religious Right Shaped Lesbian and Gay Activism*; Robinson and Spivey, "The Politics of Masculinity"; Robinson and Spivey, "Ungodly Genders."

Chapter Six

Protecting Manhood

In many ways, this book began in the fall of 2017 as I became curious about different reactions to mainstream and social media coverage of #MeToo[1] that I witnessed at various work-related events across the nation.[2] On the one hand, many of my fellow colleagues who identify as women and/or feminine talked about similar experiences to the ones appearing in the media and about the origins of the term in the mid-2000s among black women on social media sites.[3] In these conversations, mainstream media attention to #MeToo as a rallying cry and slogan felt like a welcome development. Echoing Tarana Burke's first usage of the term in 2006, it was also seen as a potential opportunity for empathy, awareness, and mobilization against patterns of racial, gendered, and sexual harassment in U.S. society. Within these conversations, #MeToo was not new, but mainstream attention to it was seen as both new and important.

On the other hand, the (mostly white and heterosexual) cisgender men I encountered at the same work events provided two different reactions to the topic. In most cases, the men in question did not bring up the subject at all despite all the news coverage or seemed to have nothing they wanted to or could say about it (when it came up, they would change the subject or move on to another conversation). In other cases, however, cisgender men appeared to want to talk about it (they would bring it up in conversation regularly), but only in the context of debating whether or not it was a good idea, dangerous, and/or a problem. These men seemed, and at times even stated that they were, worried about #MeToo and nervous about what might happen if attention to the hashtag and cases continued to grow and garner more attention.

At the time, I was working on a research project concerning the ways people in the United States respond to racial and gendered minority social movements.[4] Dr. Eric Anthony Grollman[5] had asked me this question in a conversation we had in 2015 but neither of us had much of an answer. As a result, we joined together to conduct an exploration of the topic utilizing the Black Lives Matter[6] and Transgender Bathroom Access[7] movements in the United States. As I moved from one conversation to another about #MeToo throughout 2017, I began wondering what a similar type of study might reveal about cisgender, white men's responses to #MeToo and other gendered political debates in society today. Even men who identified as liberal and/or feminist at other times seemed to feel differently regarding concrete movements both in the study I was doing on movements and during those casual conversations about #MeToo, so I became curious about what in-depth interviews on the topic would reveal regarding their thoughts and reactions.[8]

In this chapter, I return to the initial questions that led to the current study. Specifically, I outline the ways the men I interviewed made sense of minority movements seeking to challenge gendered, racial, sexual, and other inequalities[9] in U.S. society today. In so doing, I demonstrate how these men, like some of the men at the events I attended in the fall of 2017, conceptualize such movements as a challenge to manhood itself and utilize racial, gendered, and sexual stereotypes to dismiss the claims of such movements. Drawing on their own definitions of manhood as predicated on at least the threat of violent potential, the men I interviewed sought to protect their definitions of what it means to be a man by characterizing any attempt to shift or change existing social relations as a personal threat. Even when they initially expressed support for such movements, they ultimately saw attempts to shift gendered, racial, and sexual norms as problematic attempts to change how they see themselves, the world around them, and what it means to be a real man in said world.

MANHOOD AND #METOO

In order to examine how the men I interviewed responded to minority movements, I begin with the case of #MeToo and the rise of mainstream discussion of sexual harassment, sexual assault, and other violence women and femmes face throughout contemporary U.S. society today.[10] Building on and drawing from a long history of racial minority and women's rights activism, #MeToo represents one of the latest examples of political activity in search of greater gender and racial equity reaching mainstream audiences and reactions as a result of media (and in this case, social media) coverage on the issue after years of on-the-ground (and on-the-internet) mobilization, discussion, and activity.[11] In its simplest terms, #MeToo is a movement encouraging women and femmes to share their experiences with (mostly) men's sexu-

al and other harassment and violence alongside efforts to hold men accountable for such actions in the public sphere and demonstrate how widespread
such experiences are in contemporary U.S. society.

Not surprisingly, the entrance of #MeToo discussions into the mainstream
in 2017 created a social context in which all of the men I interviewed were
familiar with this hashtag and terminology. During the interviews, I sought to
understand what they thought this movement was about ("What do you think
#MeToo is seeking to accomplish?"), how they felt about the movement
("What do you think of #MeToo?"), and how this movement related to them
("How does #MeToo influence your life?"). As I did throughout the interviews, I sought to ascertain how the men I interviewed made sense of #Me-
Too in their own words rather than prompting them in any specific manner.
As there were very few interview studies about social perceptions of #MeToo
available at the time I was conducting this study, [12] I sought to ascertain what
this movement represented in the minds of cisgender, middle- and upper-
class, heterosexual white men.

The men I interviewed were split in the same way as the ones I encountered at work events. About a quarter of them (14), for example, had nothing
to say about #MeToo at all. Specifically, when asked about it, these respondents told me they "don't have anything to say about it," "don't really pay
attention to stuff like that," or "don't care about it." In these cases, follow-up
questions produced almost no elaboration. They simply sought to avoid the
topic completely rather than comment on it. In fact, it was the one place in
the interview where multiple respondents (6) asked, after two or three follow-up attempts to learn any thoughts they might have on the topic, to "move
on" or "go to the next question" instead of offering any thoughts, feelings, or
other reactions. On every other topic, however, even if they initially said they
didn't want to talk about or didn't have any thoughts on a subject, they would
elaborate when other questions made the topic relevant at some point.

One way to interpret such silence would be to assume the men in question
did not, in fact, have any opinions on the subject. However, it seems odd that
there was only one topic in the interview that they had no opinion about and
that said topic was a common point of discussion in news and other media
coverage at the time. [13] With this in mind, another way to interpret such
silence would be to view it as a form of self-protection wherein these 14 men
sought to avoid the topic by dismissing it without comment. Many of the
other men's discussions of the topic, as evidenced by this quote by a 21-year-
old Jewish man I call Simon, suggest this may have been the case: "It's not
something I like to talk about because I'm scared of saying the wrong thing.
So, I don't really talk about it at all, I just kind of ignore it. I don't want
something I say to someone now to come back at me the wrong way later,
you know what I mean?" As Simon was one of 32 men who made similar

statements, it might be that the 14 men who didn't want to speak on this one issue did, in fact, "know what" he meant.

This possibility is especially interesting for two reasons. First, the men who did speak about #MeToo generally conceptualized it as a threat predicated on the same type of "overblown" media coverage they blamed for sexual violence coverage in the media and political debates in society.[14] At the same time, however, they said many things throughout these interviews that scholars, policy makers, and others who seek to challenge or lessen violence in society would likely see as the "wrong" thing to say.[15] This begs the question as to why this was the one topic where they were afraid of saying the wrong thing. One could argue that high-profile media coverage of powerful men being held accountable as a result of #MeToo created this fear, and thus see such reactions as a result of the movement itself. Although there is no way to know for sure at present, at the very least it could be that #MeToo has created a situation where some men are afraid to openly speak about sex, gender, and sexual inequalities. If so, this would lead to other questions. Is this silence a success that may translate into changes in men's behavior, for example, or is such silence another way for men to avoid changing violent behaviors and beliefs?

Although it may be comforting to hope for the former (i.e., such silence may lead to changes in behavior), previous examples within societal debates and social science scholarship suggest the latter is more likely.[16] When silence and other manners of avoiding the topic became commonplace among whites in relation to race and racism following the civil rights movement between the 1950s and 1970s,[17] for example, this shift marked the emergence of "colorblind racism" wherein whites maintained and continued to act on long-standing racial bias while simply doing so in less explicit, quieter ways. In that case, the fear of saying the wrong thing did not result in the eradication of racial inequalities but rather transformed the ways racial inequalities were maintained and explained in social life. The men who chose not to speak on #MeToo could thus be engaging in a similar strategy whereby they are careful about what they say to protect themselves from negative reactions without necessarily changing anything about how they act or think in relation to societal patterns of sexual harassment and assault.

In fact, the responses of the men I interviewed who did talk about #MeToo also suggest this latter option may be more likely. In such cases, they typically framed #MeToo as a threat to their ideas of what a man was supposed to be and do. For example, a 24-year-old religious man I call Marty stated: "That me too stuff is just women trying to control men, that's all it is. Those guys, like the movie guy, he might have been a jerk, but he was just doing his job. What about all the people who got rich working for him? What about that? None of that matters because he liked to flirt. That's crazy." A 21-year-old atheist I call Harry added: "I think it's all a media thing. Cosby, the others, they're just rich guys so the media can make a point by putting them down. That's fine, but it's going to give these girls all the wrong ideas and I don't like that." A 24-year-old non-religious man I call Lionel added: "Me too is a joke, that's all it is. They're trying to tell guys not to be guys, yeah, that makes so much sense, it's stupid."

Rather than sexual harassment or assault (the focus of the movement), it is noteworthy that the men I interviewed saw #MeToo as a movement seeking to stop "guys" from being "guys." However, as noted in earlier chapters of this book,[18] this makes sense when people define manhood as predicated on at least potential violence. If men are violent, attempts to stop men from doing violent things (e.g., sexual harassment and sexual assault) can be seen as attempts to stop men from doing "manly" things or simply the things that make a person a man. As Randy, a 20-year-old religious man, put it:

> I think the me too thing doesn't make sense because of course men are going to flirt with women, that's a no-brainer. I think they are trying to get to the bad men who want to hurt women, but they're going about it all wrong because they're saying all the things that every guy does is bad, but that's not true. All men don't want to hurt women, they should be talking to the ones that do instead of all this stuff. I just think it doesn't make any sense. You can't tell men not to flirt or whatever it is just because there are bad guys who do crazy stuff sometimes. That's just not going to work.

Here we see the thread captured in other chapters where respondents create a "bad guy versus good guy" scheme and then suggest that attempts to oppose men's violence should focus on the bad guys, however that might be done, instead of things men do that are considered violent. In so doing, they continue to walk a mental tightrope wherein men are violent, but only some bad men that exist outside themselves are responsible for the bad version of violence.

At the same time, this was another occasion where religion seemed to play a role. Once again, however, the role of religion or non-religion involved *how* the men I interviewed explained their gender beliefs rather than what those beliefs were. Stated another way, they *believed the same thing*, but they *named different sources (religious and non-religious) as the reason for this shared belief*. Religious men, as illustrated in the following quote from a 22-year-old respondent I call Mark, saw #MeToo as an attempt to change how a supernatural deity created men to act in the world:

> I try to understand them because I realize they probably went through some bad stuff, but God created men to be like this. We are the protectors and providers; we are supposed to try to get the girl and build a family. They are the ones we pursue, and I get that sometimes bad things can happen, but you can't change the way we are created as women and men, you just try to protect yourself from the bad stuff and do the best you can.

In such cases, religious men argued that a deity created men to be the aggressors who pursue women and protect women from the pursuits of other men.[19] Since this was how men and women were created, it was natural and normal. These men saw #MeToo as attempting to use examples where "bad things" happened to try to change the way a higher power supposedly made women and men to be in the first place, which they believed was not possible.

Non-religious men, on the other hand, once again reached the same conclusion (i.e., this is just naturally the way men and women are) but drew on different ideas to explain that conclusion. In non-religious cases, as illustrated by the following quote from a 24-year-old non-religious man I call Terry, nature, or evolution, rather than a higher power was to blame:

> Harassment is just terrible, it's bad, but flirting and harassment are different things. I understand this because my sister had some issues with bad guys a couple years back. The thing is, men are going to flirt. We have to. It's in our DNA; we evolved as the ones who hunt and fight to protect others. That's just biology. We are hardwired to flirt with girls, unless we're born gay or something, it's just something we have to do, we can't control it. The harassment thing is bad, but you can't just call flirting harassment and pretend it's the same thing. That's the problem with the me too stuff, you can't fight biology, you just can't do that and expect it to work.

In non-religious cases, men thus argued that biology, DNA, and/or evolution created men to be the aggressors who pursue women and protect women from the pursuits of other men.[20] Just like their religious counterparts, the non-religious men argued that, since this was how men and women were created, it was natural and normal. Again, similar to their religious counterparts, they saw #MeToo as attempting to use examples where "terrible" or "bad" things happened to try to change the way a biological or evolutionary power supposedly made women and men to be in the first place, a change they believed was not possible.

In both cases, of course, the religious and non-religious men I interviewed are appealing to uncontrollable forces[21] to argue that the patterns of action that #MeToo advocates want to change cannot be changed. They draw on different sources of inspiration, but the results of said inspiration are the same: men are violent, something beyond men's control (e.g., God or DNA said so) and, as a result, this cannot be changed. Of course, these men are ignoring the many exceptions where people who identified as men did and do, in fact, somehow manage to resist the control of evolutionary or supernatural creators by attempting, to whatever level of success, to be non-violent and, in other cases, anti-violent in their own lives.[22] Similar to many other cases where men are presented with examples of negative or harmful behavior,[23] they interpret #MeToo as a threat and seek to define the claims of this threat as beyond their control and not their responsibility.[24] In so doing, they conceptualize the movement itself as a problem in order to maintain their own definitions of themselves as the good men who might be violent, but not in a bad way.

WHITE MANHOOD AND BLACK LIVES MATTER

Especially as #MeToo is one of many political terms and social movements that initially emerged from the efforts of black women, it is important to note, as I have at various stages throughout this book and especially in chapter 2, the role of race in societal reactions to minority movements on the one hand and movements opposing gendered and sexual violence on the other. Within this book, for example, I focus on the articulation of relationships between violence and manhood as expressed by white men. This was intentional as I sought to understand how men capable of achieving the hegemonic masculine ideal (i.e., white, class-privileged, heterosexual, cisgender) made sense of violence in society.[25] At the same time, however, whiteness as a social system plays a role in their interpretations of manhood and violence in much the same way as heterosexuality, as discussed in chapter 5. Racial influence on their definitions of manhood and violence, for example, became explicit when they discussed the "other men" who were really violent in chapter 2. Likewise, this relationship again became explicit when I asked about whiteness itself and the Black Lives Matter movement. Here, I discuss their thoughts on these latter two examples.

Although the influence of race on respondent's notions of manhood and violence only became explicit in certain cases, previous studies of relationships between race, manhood, and other social factors demonstrate the importance of race, whether or not explicitly noted, at all times for men of every racial identity.[26] Previous research, for example, might lead us to expect that non-white men would respond in similar ways to the questions discussed throughout this book because men in marginalized social locations typically learn to imitate and adopt the norms of the hegemonic masculine ideal. At the same time, however, such research might lead us to expect to get at least nuanced, and in some cases entirely different, responses from men of color to the same questions posed throughout this book as a result of the specific ways manhood, violence, and race combine within a given person's life. Although men of color in the pilot study conducted prior to this interview project expressed opinions similar to the white men in this study,[27] I caution readers not to extrapolate the findings of this study to such men. Rather, I suggest this book reveals the importance of asking all types of men about violence and the relationships between manhood and violence in U.S. society.

At the same time, it is important to recognize that whiteness, like hetero-sexuality, probably shapes much of how these respondents define manhood and its relationship to violence and other facets of their lives. Recall from chapter 2, for example, that these respondents often assumed the other, violent men that they were supposed to protect themselves and others from were men of a different race (and class). Whether or not they explicitly noted race in their discussions of "really violent" men, they could have been utilizing the same stereotypes about racial and class others each time they invoked the potential of these "really violent" men. In fact, as noted at times throughout this book, many of the ways they depict the *other violent man* they are concerned about utilize racial stereotypes and could be seen as an example of "colorblind racism"[28] when they invoke such stereotypes without explicitly saying they are talking about race. Although implicit throughout the interviews, such racial coding is more explicit when they talk about whiteness itself and their thoughts on the Black Lives Matter movement.

In the first case, I approached whiteness[29] the same way I approached manhood and heterosexuality in the interviews. Specifically, I began with an open-ended question about the subject to gather what, if anything, the men I interviewed thought about it ("You identified as white, what does it mean to be white?"). Echoing "colorblind" norms (e.g., it is not polite to talk about race; white people rarely have to discuss their own race) concerning race and racism in the United States in the past few decades, this question seemed to genuinely surprise my respondents.[30] They would typically stumble over their words at first and maybe mention or point to their skin, and then I would ask a question to try to clarify the question ("Like being a man or straight, I guess, what do you do that makes you white?" "Other than skin color, what does it mean to be white?"). In response, they would generally talk about whiteness as part of what it meant to be a man or manhood as part of being white.

This conflation between gender (manhood) and race (whiteness) implicitly defined whiteness as good (the way they defined manhood) while constructing non-whiteness as lesser (the way other gender identities were in relation to manhood).[31] Jim, a 22-year-old non-religious man, offered a typical illustration of this type of racial and gender identity construction: "Well, I guess white people are more reserved, not as emotional, and you know, a white guy takes care of his family and plays by the rules and gets a good job, I guess that's it." Brad, a 20-year-old religious man, added: "I've never thought about it, but I guess being a white man, you know, you take care of your family and your kids, you go to church, you can take care of yourself, that kind of thing." Ben, a 23-year-old Christian man, stated: "I guess it means not cool, but that's kind of dumb, you know, you do what you're supposed to do, take care of your people, you're a good guy, I don't know." Bruce, a 23-year-old non-religious man, added: "I don't know if you do anything, you just kind of are white, like you are a man, you just do normal stuff like be a good person, take care of your family, that kind of thing."

The men I interviewed were not sure how to define whiteness, but they made sure to define it as good.[32] In so doing, they utilized stereotypes of other races and associated good practices with whiteness. By defining things like taking care of your family, kids, and self (things anyone can do regardless of race) as what white people do, for example, they implicitly utilized racist stereotypes that depict people of color as less likely to do these same things to define these things as "white."[33] Likewise, by defining whiteness as "more reserved, not as emotional," respondents used elements of hegemonic manhood to define whiteness and separate it from stereotypes of women, other gender minorities, and people of color as overly emotional and less rational than white men.[34] Even more telling, Brad (and 32 other interviewees) admitted that their own whiteness—and presumably all the privileges white people have in contemporary U.S. society[35] —had never even crossed their minds.

This ability to not think about their own racial identities is especially important because whiteness, like heterosexuality and manhood, is something that has been socially constructed in different ways, at different times, and in response to various others. Likewise, it is important because people of color report the exact opposite experience—the need to develop a constant awareness of not only their own race but that of others (especially white others) they interact with throughout their lives.[36] Further, this ability to avoid thinking about race plays a heavy role in social life as research shows that racial identity—both self-reported and how others interpret us—has significant influence on every aspect of contemporary U.S. social life.[37] Finally, it is especially salient when these men respond to a movement seeking to combat societal inequalities predicated on one's social location in different racial groups.

In fact, similar to the way that racial stereotypes concerning dangerous men of color emerged as the men I interviewed sought to define who they would need to protect themselves and others from, discussed in chapter 2, negative assumptions about non-white people arose throughout their discussions of Black Lives Matter.[38] As in other cases, however, all I asked was what they thought about the movement ("What do you think about Black Lives Matter?") without any qualification or attempt to lead the conversation in a certain direction. Rather than a movement, however, they generally saw Black Lives Matter as, to quote a 20-year-old atheist I call Danny, "A problem, that's what it is. All lives matter, everyone knows that. What they're trying to do is attack hard-working cops who protect all of us." A 19-year-old Christian man I call Bryan offered a similar take: "My dad says they're a bunch of terrorists, but I don't think it's that bad. It's more like a bunch of troublemakers who don't want to act right, that's my take."

The men I interviewed conceptualized Black Lives Matter as a threat. Sometimes, they defined it as a threat to police. Other times it was a threat to behavioral norms (e.g., how people should act or do politics). Other times, as illustrated by the following quote from a non-religious 22-year-old I call Adrian, it was a threat to the United States itself: "They are just making a lot of noise, they want to divide the country, that's what it seems like, they want to make everything about race like it was in the past." Other times, as illustrated by a 22-year-old Christian man I call Jacob, it was a threat to themselves specifically: "Look, I get that things are not the best, but riots and stuff like that won't help and it might get a lot of people hurt. I don't want to get caught up in some crazy stuff that don't involve me just because I'm walking down the street." Regardless of what they thought it threatened, the conceptualization of Black Lives Matter—like their definition of other men who are violent—was almost entirely in terms of a threat to some aspect of contemporary norms in the United States.

It was also, as suggested by the last quote above, something they saw as separate from their own lives.[39] Rather than seeing Black Lives Matter's calls for racial equity in relation to their own privilege as white Americans, they saw the movement as a separate entity that did not have anything to do with them. Lee, a 21-year-old Christian man, offered a typical example of this line of thinking: "I try not to think about it, I mean I know it's happening, but it has nothing to do with me, it's their thing, so I just mind my business because I don't like it, but it doesn't really affect me anyway." Lucas, a 19-year-old non-religious man, sounded a similar note: "They're trying to make a point, but I don't really know what it is because it doesn't really have anything to do with me." The same way their own whiteness was something they could take for granted without much consideration, they were able to avoid and ignore attempts by others to pursue better treatment for another race without much consideration.

MANHOOD AND MOVEMENTS

Throughout this section, I utilized the cases of the #MeToo and Black Lives Matter movements to examine how the men I interviewed react to movements seeking to change existing sexual, racial, and gendered inequalities in U.S. society. Specifically, I outlined the ways they defined such movements as a threat to themselves and to manhood itself. At the same time, however, I explored the ways they constructed whiteness as a moral identity,[40] or an identity that grants moral worth and value to a human being regardless of any concrete action on the part of the person. In so doing, I demonstrated how their own perspectives as white men facilitated their depiction of racial justice movements as threats to their own standing that simultaneously had nothing to do with them personally. Finally, I documented the ways they define movements seeking social change as threats to their own abilities to maintain their current gendered, racial, sexual, and behavior norms as white, cisgender heterosexual men.

Although the space limitations of any book or chapter require the selection of cases to illustrate any given concept or idea, it is important to note that #MeToo and Black Lives Matter were not the only movements I asked my respondents about in the interviews. Even so, their reactions to these movements were about the same as their reactions to, for example, transgender rights movements; lesbian, gay, and bisexual rights movements; and women's movements seeking access to abortion or changes to the pay gap between women and men.[41] Put simply, they saw any movement that sought to change existing norms between white, cisgender, heterosexual men and other social groups as a threat to both themselves personally and manhood itself. Rather than considering the possibility that such movements could make things better for more people or even have positive impacts on themselves personally, they interpreted such efforts as problematic attempts by others to control how they lived and experienced their own lives as men. In so doing, they implicitly argued that the conservation of manhood predicated on control and violence was more important than any inequalities that existing social relationships created and maintained for other groups of people.

The findings in this chapter also bring us back to the questions at the beginning of this book: what does it mean to be a man, how does violence relate to definitions of manhood, and how do men respond to attempts to change social norms? Throughout this chapter and the ones preceding it, the answer remains the same. First, manhood is defined in terms of the ability to control self and others, protect self and others, and use at least the threat of violence when necessary to maintain control or protection. Second, violence is defined as a way men may respond when they lose—or even feel they lose—control in any aspect of life. Third, manhood itself, as well as its requirements for violent potential, must be protected against attempts to change it in any way (e.g., take control of it). In each case, my respondents argue that men must be violent to protect themselves and others from violent other men and/or attempts by other groups to change existing social relations that privilege men over other groups.

This focus on protection has implications for any attempt to understand manhood and violence in society. If there are always other violent men out there somewhere, for example, then men must be prepared to use violence at any moment in response to such others. At the same time, however, this means that anyone can be defined as one of the violent men out there in order for men to justify violence against others. Likewise, if other gender, racial, and sexual groups are a threat to men anytime they pursue better treatment as individuals or within movements, then men must be prepared to exercise control in any case where they encounter others. This means that any attempt by sexual, gender, or racial minorities to challenge inequalities can be defined as simply an attack on men, one that men should dismiss and/or oppose. In all such cases, the men I interviewed always have a ready explanation for violence as well as reasons to avoid changing anything about themselves or manhood in general. In the concluding chapter, I explore the implications of these findings for relationships between manhood and violence throughout U.S. society today.

NOTES

1. #MeToo is a social movement started in 2006 by Tarana Burke to highlight the specific experiences of girls of color with sexual violence. In 2017, the hashtag #MeToo was widely circulated on Twitter and other social media platforms to draw attention to Harvey Weinstein's sexually violent and predatory behavior toward women. Since then, #MeToo has become a popular hashtag and phrase used by survivors of sexual violence to illustrate the pervasiveness of this issue. See *Time* magazine's "Our Pain Is Never Prioritized" for more information.

2. Some of these events were on my own campus, others were at community organizations, and others were at conferences I attended with other scholars in the social sciences.

3. See note 1.

4. See Sumerau, Forbes, Grollman, and Mathers, "Constructing Allyship," and Sumerau and Grollman, "Obscuring Oppression." Additionally, my colleague and I are also currently composing a book on this project for publication in the near future.

5. For more on Dr. Grollman's work, visit their website at https://egrollman.com.

6. Carruthers, *Unapologetic*; Khan-Cullors and bandele, *When They Call You a Terrorist*; Ray, "If Only He Didn't Wear the Hoodie." See also https://blacklivesmatter.com.

7. Mathers, "Bathrooms, Boundaries, and Emotional Burdens"; Schilt and Westbrook, "Bathroom Battlegrounds and Penis Panics"; Stone, "Gender Panics about Transgender Children"; Westbrook and Schilt, "Doing Gender, Determining Gender."

8. See the methodological appendix for more information.

9. Most movements focus on multiple issues at a time. For further reading on intersectional politics, movements, and issues see Collins, *Black Feminist Thought*; Cottom, *Thick;* Crenshaw, "Mapping the Margins"; and Gay, *Not That Bad*.

10. Martin, "'Said and Done' versus 'Saying and Doing'"; Moloney and Love, "Assessing Online Misogyny"; Sweet, "Sociology of Gaslighting." See chapter 3, note 2 for recent examples of such cases.

11. Collins, *Black Feminist Thought*; Combahee River Collective, "A Black Feminist Statement"; Rich, "Compulsory Heterosexuality"; Smith, *The Everyday World as Problematic.*

12. But see Hassan, Mandal, Bhuiyan, Moitra, and Ahmed, "Nonparticipation of Bangladeshi Women in #MeToo Movement." Aside from this study, the author is aware of no studies that address the perceptions of #MeToo through the use of interview data.

13. Codrea-Rado, "#MeToo Floods Social Media"; Gilbert, "The Movement of #MeToo"; Khomani, "#MeToo: How a Hashtag Became a Rallying Cry"; Rogers, "#MeToo: How an 11-Year-Old Movement Became a Social Media Phenomenon."

14. See the discussions in chapters 3 and 5.

15. See Bonilla-Silva, *Racism without Racists*; Connell, *Gender and Power*; Gay, *Not That Bad*; Martin, *Rape Work*; Sumerau and Cragun, *Christianity and the Limits of Minority Acceptance*; Sumerau and Mathers, *America through Transgender Eyes*; and Friedman and Valenti, *Yes Means Yes!*, for examples of discussions of inequalities.

16. Bonilla-Silva, *Racism without Racists*; Mathers, Sumerau, and Cragun, "The Limits of Homonormativity"; Pascoe and Hollander, "Good Guys Don't Rape"; Sumerau et al., "Constructing Allyship."

17. Alexander, *The New Jim Crow*; Barber and Bridges, "Marketing Manhood in a 'Post-Feminist' Age"; Bonilla-Silva, *Racism without Racists*; Collins, *Black Feminist Thought*; Collins, *Black Sexual Politics*; Sumerau and Grollman, "Obscuring Oppression."

18. See especially chapter 5.

19. Pitt, "Killing the Messenger"; Sumerau, "That's What a Man Is Supposed to Do"; Sumerau, Cragun, and Mathers, "Contemporary Religion and the Cisgendering of Reality"; Sumerau, Cragun, and Mathers, "I Found God in the Glory Hole"; Thumma, "Negotiating a Religious Identity."

20. See Connell and Messerschmidt, "Hegemonic Masculinity," and Schrock and Schwalbe, "Men, Masculinity, and Manhood Acts," for evidence that challenges this line of thinking. Unfortunately, current studies of non-religion typically focus on relationships between theism (i.e., belief in a higher power) versus non-theisim (i.e., non-belief in the supernatural) but rarely discuss anything related to race, class, gender, or sexual beliefs and behaviors of the non-religious (Smith and Cragun, "Mapping Religion's Other"). However, studies of the non-religious have demonstrated that most of the people in such populations, at present, tend to be white, cisgender, heterosexual, class-privileged men like the ones I interviewed for this study. As I discuss in the concluding chapter, this raises questions about what, if anything, separates religious and non-religious belief beyond questions about the existence of a higher power? At present, however, there is no way to know what the answers to this question might be.

21. See Scott and Lyman, "Accounts."

22. For example, see *Tough Guise* and *Tough Guise 2* as well as anti-violence efforts such as the organization Mentors in Violence Prevention developed by Jackson Katz.

23. See Cragun and Sumerau, "Losing Manhood Like a Man," for an example and review.

24. Schrock, McCabe, and Vacarro, "Narrative Manhood Acts"; Schrock and Padavic, "Negotiating Hegemonic Masculinity."

25. Connell and Messerschmidt, "Hegemonic Masculinity."

26. For examples of such research, see chapter 2, note 10.

27. See the methodological appendix for more information.

28. Bonilla-Silva, *Racism without Racists.*

29. Doane and Bonilla-Silva, *White Out*; Feagin, *The White Racial Frame*; McDermott and Samson, "White Racial and Ethnic Identity."

30. See Bonilla-Silva, *Racism without Racists.*

31. Buggs, "Color, Culture, or Cousin?"; Buggs, "Dating in the Time of #BlackLivesMatter"; Collins, *Black Sexual Politics*; Cottom, *Lower Ed*; Cottom, *Thick*; Espiritu, "We Don't Sleep Around Like White Girls Do"; Ferguson, *Aberrations in Black*; Garcia, *Respect Yourself*; Snorton, *Black on Both Sides*; Washington, *Medical Apartheid*; Wingfield, "Racializing the Glass Escalator."

32. Omi and Winant, *Racial Formation in the United States.*

33. See Ray, "If Only He Didn't Wear the Hoodie," on racial stereotypes.

34. Collins, *Black Feminist Thought*; Jackson and Wingfield, "Getting Angry to Get Ahead"; Wingfield, "The Modern Mammy and the Angry Black Man."

35. See the citations in note 29.

36. For examples, see Cooper, *Eloquent Rage*; Cottom, *Thick*; Gay, *Bad Feminist*; Khan-Cullors and bandele, *When They Call You a Terrorist*; Mock, *Redefining Realness.*

37. Bor, Venkataramani, Williams, and Tsai, "Police Killings and Their Spillover Effects"; Reskin, "The Race Discrimination System"; Sewell, "The Racism-Race Reification Process"; Washington, *Medical Apartheid.*

38. Ray, Brown, Summers, and Fraistat, "Ferguson and the Death of Michael Brown"; Sumerau and Grollman, "Obscuring Oppression."

39. Fields, "Normal Queers"; Mathers, Sumerau, and Ueno, "This Isn't Just Another Gay Group"; Sumerau et al., "Constructing Allyship."

40. Katz, "Essences as Moral Identities"; Kleinman, *Opposing Ambitions*; Mathers, Sumerau, and Ueno, "This Isn't Just Another Gay Group"; Ueno and Gentile, "Moral Identity in Friendships."

41. Coley, *Gay on God's Campus*; Rohlinger, *Abortion Politics, Mass Media, and Social Movements*; Stryker, *Transgender History.*

Conclusion

Although I never planned to study men and masculinities when I entered graduate school in the fall of 2008,[1] my interests in understanding societal patterns of inequality and violence have repeatedly led me to these topics throughout my research career to date. When I was in graduate school seeking to understand how LGBT Christians made sense of religion, sexualities, and gender in the southeastern United States, for example, I was struck by patterns wherein some gay men within this population sought to compensate for their subordination versus ideal notions of heterosexual manhood and the impact such efforts had on the rest of the community.[2] Likewise, as I worked on studies examining how cisgender college students in the United States made sense of bisexual, polyamorous, transgender, and racial minority populations in recent years,[3] I repeatedly encountered many ways their (often negative) reactions to such groups connected to their beliefs about what it meant to be a man or woman and the ways such meanings influenced beliefs about other sex, gender, sexual, and racial populations.

As I noted in the opening section of chapter 6, I became especially aware of these patterns in the fall of 2017 as men around me—regardless of how they identified politically or otherwise—reacted to increased societal attention to #MeToo. Although I had written extensively about sex, gender, and sexualities for years and published multiple works on relationships between manhood, inequalities, and violence by that point in my career, I realized that I had never explicitly designed a study with the express purpose of understanding the construction and operation of men and masculinities in society.[4] It was this realization that led to the study at the heart of this book. As I noted in chapter 1, I sought to understand how people who identify as men define what it means to be a man. Further, I wanted to learn, in their own words, how men defined potential relationships between manhood and violence.

Throughout this book, I have utilized the responses of the men I interviewed to answer these questions. Specifically, I demonstrated how they defined manhood as predicated upon the ability to protect themselves and others from (mostly) other men. Likewise, I outlined how their conceptualization of men as protectors from threats, and other men as threats to be protected against, define violence—or at least the possibility of enacting it—as a necessary component of what it means to be a man. Further, I discussed the ways this creation of violence as part of manhood, and manhood as necessarily violent, finds voice in their attempts to dismiss societal violence by excusing forms of it they do not expect to experience and justifying forms of it they can expect themselves to face. Finally, I showed how their own conflation of manhood and violence finds voice in the ways they define themselves in racial and sexual terms as well as the ways they respond to efforts by others to challenge violence in society. Overall, I have argued throughout this book that understanding—and thus changing—violence in society requires deconstructing and changing what it means to be a man in the United States today.

To this end, I utilize this chapter to draw out implications of these findings for scholarship concerning sex, gender, and sexualities; men and masculinities; and violence in contemporary U.S. society. In so doing, I seek to provide pathways for researchers, policy makers, activists, elected officials, and other members of U.S. society who seek to make sense of and potentially change existing relationships between violence and manhood in society. Further, I seek to encourage researchers studying men and masculinities on the one hand, and violence itself on the other hand, to integrate their efforts in hopes of fostering data-based interventions to violence in contemporary society. Finally, I utilize these concluding remarks to encourage and facilitate continued theoretical, empirical, and political attention to ongoing societal conversations about what it means to be a man, what impact such meanings have on violence, and what factors may contribute to lessening men's violence over time.

WHAT IT MEANS TO BE A MAN AS A
FUNDAMENTAL CAUSE OF VIOLENCE

Alongside gender and sexualities, I often study inequalities in health and medical access. Within such work, I focus on what scholars refer to as "fundamental causes" of health.[5] Put simply, "fundamental causes" of health refer to the social factors that determine what groups of people (e.g., the poor or racial minorities) are more likely to experience negative health outcomes as a result of social inequalities (e.g., poverty or racism) regardless of any individual factors.[6] Stated another way, interdisciplinary health research within and beyond sociology demonstrates that social factors can fundamentally cause specific health outcomes and inequalities because a person's location within a given social context or group will impact their health no matter what said person does individually in their own personal life. Social factors thus put some population groups within a society at greater risk of individually facing or developing risky or negative health behaviors, attitudes, experiences, or expectations.

In fact, some gender scholarship has already begun to demonstrate that gender itself is often a fundamental cause of health inequalities.[7] When doctors are less likely to take seriously the symptoms or other information provided by women and transgender people (and especially people of color who are also women and/or transgender people), for example, said doctors are responding to the gender (and often race) of the patient in ways that make those patients less likely to gain necessary treatment and care at the same speed as men.[8] Likewise, when transgender populations are both more likely to have insurance for medical care and also less likely to find doctors willing to provide them with the care, their gender, rather than any individual aspect of their lives, creates potential problems for their overall health and access to medical care.[9] In these and other cases, the way people interpret and respond to gender itself fundamentally causes unequal health and medical outcomes for members of certain gender groups.

Although the observations above are fairly standard within interdisciplinary health studies at present, the concept of "fundamental causes" may be relevant in many areas beyond health and medicine. As illustrated throughout this book, one of these areas may be violence. If, for example, people define what it means to be a man as necessarily violent, then manhood may be seen as a fundamental cause of violence in society. Stated another way, if men are taught they must at least be ready and willing to engage in violence, we have already created manhood in a way that makes men's violence more likely no matter what an individual man intends.[10] Likewise, if we have already trained men to see other men as necessarily and automatically violent, we again have created manhood in a way that makes men's violence—or at least their ability to accept, justify, excuse, and enact violence—more likely regardless of the intentions of any individual who identifies as a man.[11] Put simply, if violence is defined as a necessary part of being a man, then this definition of manhood (i.e., violent is what it means to be a man) itself becomes a fundamental cause of violence in society.

Of course, my point here is not that manhood has to be violent or that all violence is fundamentally caused by current definitions of what it means to be a man.[12] Rather, the point is that definitions of manhood that require violence will necessarily require men to become at least potentially violent and accepting of violence to show themselves and others that they are, in fact, really men. If, however, manhood is defined as not necessarily violent or if violence is defined as opposite to manhood, then men's violence might become less likely, less understandable, less easily excused or justified and, in short, less normal.[13] Stated another way, the same way that reducing racism or poverty would facilitate fewer racial and class inequalities in the health of racial minorities and poor people, challenging definitions of manhood that require violence as part of that definition would facilitate lower likelihoods of men engaging in, supporting, and otherwise celebrating violence. The point here is that if we seek to curb, much less change, societal patterns of men's violence against themselves and others, we need to take a tip from health sciences. This would involve focusing on the fundamental causes (in this case, being a man involves being violent) that *initially place* men at risk of being violent *before* any individual man enters a scenario in which he might find it reasonable to engage in violence.

To accomplish this, however, we would need to challenge every excuse or justification mobilized to dismiss men's violence against themselves and others. We would further need to redefine violence as something negative, wrong, and inexcusable throughout our society through the use of media, religion, education, and other representations of what it means to be a member of a given society. Although this may sound extremely unlikely to many of us situated within the current historical moment, we must remember that these same resources have been mobilized at different times in history to justify, excuse, and encourage men's violence;[14] facilitate and justify discrimination against every minority group in society;[15] and encourage the adoption of specific behaviors that were once thought of as impossible at a given time.[16] Rather than continuing endless cycles of debate about what individual factors (e.g., biology or mental illness) might explain societal violence or the multitude of ways we might categorize "masculinity" in various settings and populations, we could challenge the definition of manhood as violent that may fundamentally cause—or at least allow—men's violence in society.

COMPENSATORY VIOLENCE/MANHOOD

To this end, we need to return to the central premise illustrated throughout this book: that violence is a way that men may compensate for situations where they feel they have lost control of themselves and others. Examining decades of scholarship on men and masculinities, Schrock and Schwalbe[17] defined control as a central element of what it means to be a man in the United States today. In fact, even the conceptualization provided by the men I interviewed (men as protectors) suggests that manhood is built on controlling something (the outcomes of themselves or others in relation to potential negative events). With this in mind, researchers have consistently demonstrated that people who identify as men and either (1) experience a lack of control in society due to race, class, sex, sexual, or other marginalization, or (2) experience a lack of control in their own lives due to illness, confinement, or other factors seek to compensate for this perceived loss of control by emphasizing elements of manhood including but not limited to violence against the self and others.[18] The combination of these insights suggests that violence represents a way for men who lack other ways to demonstrate control to re-establish at least the perception, within themselves and among others, that they can take control.

As I've argued throughout this book, this observation has broader implications because any man, no matter his other demographic or contextual characteristics, will face situations where he feels out of control of himself or others. This, of course, is part of the human experience; much of our lives are experienced within contexts where we have, at most, only limited amounts of control over anything. For men, however, this means that much of their lives are experienced in contexts that threaten their manhood, at least to an extent.[19] In previous generations and contexts, for example, such men might utilize their greater economic, sexual, or other privileges to signify power and control.[20] These privileges were generally written into the laws of the nation, and history is full of examples of violent reactions whenever such laws were challenged or changed. In such cases, the emergence of greater rights and opportunities for other gender (and race and sexual) populations shifted the prior dynamic. Many men are not economically, sexually, or in any other way powerful or in control at present. In such cases, violence remains the thing all men can access to signify control over themselves and others at any given time and in any given situation.

As noted throughout this book, the question then is which men will utilize violence to compensate in situations where they feel their manhood threatened by a lack or lessening amount of control over self and others? Since violence is defined by men as a fundamental or necessary part of being a man,[21] there is no way to tell in advance whether a given individual man will utilize violence as a compensatory strategy. There is also no way to predict if said men will use structural, interpersonal, physical, emotional, or other forms of violence if or when they seek to compensate for feelings of inadequacy, however real or imagined, in their own lives. Although researchers often view compensation as an element of only men in subordinated social locations, it is equally necessary to examine how men in all social locations compensate for perceived threats to manhood. In fact, this type of analysis, as suggested throughout this book, may be a key to uncovering fundamental elements of both violence and manhood at work throughout a given society.

However, this possibility also raises another question: What happens if we redefine manhood as oppositional to violence? Would it still represent a viable compensatory act for men who feel out of control in some way?

Would it instead be replaced with some other way (e.g., caring for children, cleaning up the environment, or any other thing we could socially define as what it means to be a man) for them to compensate in situations where they felt less manly? These, of course, are open questions with only hypothetical answers. At the same time, they demonstrate the usefulness of critically examining the relationships between what it means to be a man and the ways men act to show themselves and others that they really are men. At present, one way they can do this is by enacting violence to (re)establish at least the appearance of control, but if violence and manhood were socially decoupled, this option might change.

As a result, the analyses throughout this book suggest an important site of research, advocacy, policy, and other efforts to reduce violence in society and involve attempts to understand men's definitions of what it means to be a man and the ways men may seek to compensate for situations wherein they feel such definitions threatened. In this way, we might move past documenting and predicting the next batch of violent headlines and instead focus our attention on seeking to shift the meanings of violence, manhood, and men's violence that give rise to such headlines in the first place. To this end, we may need to focus on the fact that even if "not all men" will necessarily commit violence, we have created a version of ideal or hegemonic manhood in the United States wherein "all men" might at any time commit violence and where all non-men must be ready for the possibility that any man could be the next one to compensate with violence for perceived loss of status.

THE VARIETIES OF VIOLENT MANHOOD

Although the points above direct our attention to the shared relationships between men's gender identities and violence revealed by the men I interviewed, it is also important to recognize how other social locations, such as race and sexualities, impact what it means to be a man and thus the methods whereby men may seek to signify their manhood to others. As scholars of intersectionality have long noted,[22] this means we must remain focused on the ways race, class, gender, sexualities, and other social locations are always being constructed, maintained, and transformed in relationship to one another. Although researchers typically focus attention on members of marginalized groups,[23] the analysis throughout this book reminds us of the importance of also focusing on the meaning-making efforts of members of privileged groups.

Specifically, the men I interviewed occupied privileged racial, classed, gendered, and sexual social locations that impacted both how they defined manhood itself and how they defined race, class, and sexuality. When they defined what it meant to be white, for example, they constructed whiteness as a category characterized by moral value and positive qualities. At the same time, however, they often defined racial minority men as threatening and otherwise negative or immoral. In this way, they reproduced white privilege and supremacy in their own definitions of white men as good men and men of color as potentially dangerous threats they had to be ready to protect themselves and others from throughout their lives. As a result, their conceptualization of manhood and whiteness both contained the seeds for excusing and justifying violence against non-white men and members of other gender groups regardless of race or ethnicity. The analysis here thus demonstrates the importance of ascertaining not only how men define what it means to be a man, but also how they do so in racialized ways that may reproduce the marginalization of people of color.[24]

We saw a similar relationship in the case of sexuality when the men I interviewed constructed their own heterosexual identities as necessarily violent. Although heterosexual violence and violent manhood could operate in separate ways, these two factors, alongside whiteness, came together in the ways the men I interviewed made sense of violence against cisgender heterosexual women and LGBT communities. Further, their elaboration of what it means to be heterosexual men suggested that sexual violence itself was a normal element of their sexual identities rather than any kind of problem. As in the case of racial meanings, their discussions of sexualities direct attention to the importance of examining not only manhood but how men construct heterosexuality and heterosexual manhood in relation to violence. As suggested by emerging critical studies of heterosexuality,[25] such analyses may reveal tremendous insights into relationships between gender, sexualities, and violence that must be uncovered and deconstructed as part of attempts to reduce sexual violence in society.

We can hypothesize a similar situation in relation to class variation. Although all the men I interviewed were from middle- and upper-class backgrounds, for example, they often characterized poor and working-class men as the real violent and dangerous men. This was, as noted in chapter 2, similar to their depictions of men of color. At the same time, however, they generally exhibited a lack of understanding when I asked what it meant to be middle or upper class. Rather than being able to define their own class identities the way they did with manhood (gender identity), heterosexuality (sexual identity), and whiteness (racial identity), they were almost entirely silent on what it meant to be a member of a given class. This, I would suggest, is a limitation of the current study. I did not push harder for discussions of class identities, but future research should pursue this topic. Especially considering the ways they defined racial and sexual identities, such study could reveal important components of relationships between manhood and violence as well as relationships between these phenomena, sexuality, and race.[26]

Within this study, however, questions about intersections between manhood, violence, and other social locations raise unanswered theoretical questions in the case of religious and non-religious identities. As noted in chapter 2, some research suggests significant variation (often captured via statistical methods) between religious men and others in terms of gender beliefs, values, and assumptions,[27] but other research suggests religious and non-religious men respond in similar ways to questions about gender in society.[28] In this case, the latter option showed up no matter the topic in question. Although religious men and non-religious men cited different authorities (e.g., religious scripture and deities in the former case; scientific arguments and leaders in the latter case), they overwhelmingly expressed the exact same gender beliefs.

Since scientists have not yet begun to do comparative studies of religious and non-religious men focused on their racial, classed, sexed, gendered, sexual, or other beliefs,[29] it is not yet possible to say what exactly the similarities between religious and non-religious men in this study might mean in a broader sense. Rather, what this study does is suggest that it may already be time for recently emerging non-religious or secular studies to incorporate critical studies of inequalities into their work. At present, however, most secular or non-religious studies (1) assume that differences in belief in a deity (i.e., whether there is a god or higher power) lead to different beliefs about other social factors (e.g., race, class, gender, sexuality), or (2) limit their focus to comparisons of religious and non-religious populations to issues like family formation, religious/secular identity development, secular/religious organizational or movement formation, and health outcomes. What might examinations of the race, class, sex, gender, or sexual beliefs among non-religious populations look like? How similar or different might they be from their religious counterparts?

These questions may also lead scholars focused on secular or non-religious experiences and populations to be careful about the interpretation of surveys. As researchers have shown in relation to race, gender, class, and sexualities in recent years,[30] people often say one thing about inequalities in a survey (e.g., I oppose racism), but then reveal different and even opposite beliefs about the same topic in an in-depth interview (I oppose racism, but there are things . . .). Considering that much of the research on non-religious groups to date is survey based, hypothesized liberal leanings in relation to political issues may be a byproduct of the methodology rather than any real variation or difference from religious populations. This is, of course, an empirical question, but the similarities between the religious and non-religious men I interviewed suggest it is an important one for researchers to address. Only then may we learn what, if any, variations emerge among religious and non-religious populations when it comes to relationships between violence and manhood in contemporary U.S. society.

Of course, these are only a few of the potential varieties of manhood that may or may not reveal different definitions of what it means to be a man and what ways violence finds voice in such definitions. Researchers studying, for example, variations and intersections related to age, disability, marital status, relationship preferences, local and global regions, and many other factors may contribute to the conversation in a wide variety of ways. The point, however, remains the same: Understanding relationships between violence and manhood also requires examining intersections between manhood, violence, and the other social locations occupied by people who identify as men. In so doing, researchers could develop more complete and robust portraits of the varieties of what it means to be a man and the collection of potential relationships between violence and manhood within and between social groups.

CONCLUDING REMARKS

As I complete this book, I think about the different ways I am treated when people interpret my presentation of self as potential manhood, womanhood, or some space between and beyond these options. As I noted in chapter 1, these varied situations consistently remind me of the importance of how people define what it means to be a man, a woman, or neither of these gender identities, and the consequences that arise in response to such definitions. Rather than abstract categories contained within this or other written works, the ways people define and interpret gender have real-world consequences that influence every aspect of contemporary social life. It is with this in mind that the importance of ascertaining how people individually and collectively construct such meanings becomes clear.

Throughout this book, I have sought to offer an example of such an effort. Whether in relation to themselves or others, the men I interviewed defined manhood as necessarily involving at least the potential for violence. At the same time, they excused and justified violence in the broader society as a way to maintain these definitions of manhood and in response to their own recognition that violence, regardless of how it was defined, could be a way to compensate for perceived threats to manhood. In so doing, their own words demonstrate that rather than separate arenas for analysis and consideration, violence and manhood are conceptual terrains that often overlap in ways such that seeking to change one will necessitate changing the other. Although transforming definitions of manhood predicated on violence may be a tall order, the men I interviewed suggest it will be a necessary endeavor if we truly seek to create a less violent world with more equity and opportunity for all.

NOTES

1. I actually entered graduate school planning to study adoption, LGBT studies, and the culture of the southeastern United States because I was interested in understanding my own biographical and regional background. I have continued to study each of these topics as well as health throughout my career, but during graduate school, the data I found in my study of southeastern LGBT Christian churches led me to focus heavily on gender and masculinities at the time.

2. Sumerau, "Some of Us Are Good"; Sumerau, "Somewhere between Evangelical and Queer"; Sumerau, "That's What a Man Is Supposed to Do"; Sumerau, Cragun, and Mathers, "I Found God in the Glory Hole"; Sumerau, Padavic, and Schrock, "Little Girls Unwilling to Do."

3. Mathers, Sumerau, and Cragun, "The Limits of Homonormativity"; McCabe and Sumerau, "Reproductive Vocabularies"; Sumerau and Cragun, *Christianity and the Limits*; Sumerau, Forbes, Grollman, and Mathers, "Constructing Allyship"; Sumerau and Grollman, "Obscuring Oppression"; Sumerau and Mathers, *America through Transgender Eyes*; Sumerau, Mathers, and Moon, "Foreclosing Fluidity at the Intersection of Gender and Sexual Normativities."

4. See the methodological appendix for more on study design.

5. Harder and Sumerau, "Understanding Gender as a Fundamental Cause of Health"; Nowakowski and Sumerau, "Aging Partners Managing Chronic Illness"; Nowakowski and Sumerau, *Negotiating the Emotional Challenges*; Nowakowski and Sumerau, "Out of the Shadows"; Nowakowski and Sumerau, "Reframing Health and Illness"; Nowakowski and Sumerau, "Should We Talk about the Pain?"

6. Link and Phelan, "Social Conditions as Fundamental Causes of Disease"; Miller and Grollman, "The Social Costs of Gender Nonconformity"; Nowakowski and Sumerau, "Aging Partners"; Pirtle, "Racial Capitalism: A Fundamental Cause"; Sewell, "The Racism-Race Reification Process."

7. Calasanti and Slevin, *Gender, Social Inequalities, and Aging*; Harder and Sumerau, "Understanding Gender"; Nowakowski and Sumerau, "Swell Foundations."

8. Calasanti and Slevin, *Gender, Social Inequalities, and Aging*; Sumerau and Mathers, *America through Transgender Eyes*; Washington, *Medical Apartheid.*

9. Johnson, "Normative Accountability"; shuster, "Uncertain Expertise and the Limitations of Clinical Guidelines"; Sumerau and Mathers, *America through Transgender Eyes.*

10. See also Schrock and Schwalbe, "Men, Masculinity, and Manhood Acts."

11. Pierce, Schrock, Erichsen, and Dowd-Arrow, "Valorizing Trump's Masculine Self."

12. Rather, one could argue that manhood, as currently defined, is one of many fundamental causes of violence in society alongside current social definitions of, for example, whiteness (Sewell, "Racism-Race Reification"), heterosexuality (Schrock, Sumerau, and Ueno, "Sexualities"), and other systems that benefit some groups at the expense of others.

13. Messner, *Guys Like Me.*

14. Pascoe and Bridges, *Exploring Masculinities*; Schrock and Schwalbe, "Men, Masculinity, and Manhood Acts."

15. Collins, *Black Sexual Politics*; Foucault, *Discipline and Punish*; Johnson, *The Gender Knot*; Schrock, Sumerau, and Ueno, "Sexualities"; Sumerau and Mathers, *America through Transgender Eyes*; Warner, *The Trouble with Normal.*

16. Sanders, Antin, Hunt, and Young, "Is Smoking Queer?" See, for example, the dramatic decrease in smoking over the past few decades as a result of media, political, and education campaigns defining this once normal activity as deviant and abnormal in society now.

17. Schrock and Schwalbe, "Men, Masculinity, and Manhood Acts." See also Ezzell, "I'm in Control"; Sumerau, "That's What a Man."

18. See again, Ezzell, "I'm in Control"; Schrock, McCabe, and Vaccaro, "Narrative Manhood Acts"; Schrock and Padavic, "Negotiating Hegemonic Masculinity."

19. Connell, *Gender and Power*; Martin, "Mobilizing Masculinities"; Schrock and Padavic, "Negotiating Hegemonic Masculinity."

20. Connell, *Gender and Power*; Johnson, *The Gender Knot.*

21. See also Connell, *Gender and Power*; Schrock and Schwalbe, "Men, Masculinity, and Manhood Acts."

22. Collins, *Black Feminist Thought*; Combahee River Collective, "A Black Feminist Statement"; Crenshaw, "Mapping the Margins."

23. Collins, *Intersectionality as Critical Social Theory*; Schwalbe, Godwin, Holden, Schrock, Thompson, and Wolkomir, "Generic Processes in the Reproduction of Inequality."

24. Anderson, *Code of the Street*; Collins, *Intersectionality*.

25. Katz, *The Invention of Heterosexuality*; Pascoe, *Dude, You're a Fag*.

26. Collins, *Intersectionality*; Cottom, *Lower Ed*; Crenshaw, "Mapping the Margins."

27. Cragun and Sumerau, "No One Expects a Transgender Jew"; Kolysh, "Straight Gods, White Devils"; Mathers, "Expanding on the Experiences of Transgender Nonreligious People."

28. Cragun and Sumerau, "No One Expects"; Sumerau and Cragun, *Christianity and the Limits of Minority Acceptance in America*; Sumerau and Mathers, *America through Transgender Eyes*.

29. In a recent review of the emerging field of non-religious and secular studies, for example, these topics are not among the areas considered part of this new field (Smith and Cragun, "Mapping Religion's Other"), but see Dunn and Creek, "Identity Dilemmas," and Stewart, Frost, and Edgell, "Intersectionality and Power," for exceptions.

30. See, for example, Bonilla-Silva, *Racism without Racists*.

Methodological Appendix

As noted in chapter 6, the seeds of this book were planted in a series of interactions I had with colleagues and others in the fall of 2017. At the time, the #MeToo movement was beginning to gain mainstream attention,[1] and I became struck by the different ways people responded to this development in a movement that had been active for more than a decade. As I was analyzing data and pursuing publications from other projects examining how people responded to minority groups and movements as well as the experiences of transgender people in society, I started to think that maybe my next study should focus specifically on the ways people who identified as men reacted to #MeToo, other social movements, and debates related to sex, gender, and sexualities, and violence in society more broadly. At the time, I wasn't sure what, if anything, I might find in such a study.

Especially because I didn't know what I might want to ask or what I might find studying men's definitions of themselves and others, I designed a preliminary, or pilot, study as an opportunity to get a basic idea of what such an endeavor might reveal.[2] As a non-binary transgender woman, I was uncertain how people who identified as men would make sense of any political topics, much less political issues specifically tied to sex, gender, and sexualities. I had some hunches from my experiences navigating interactions with men, and studying men and masculinities as part of other projects, but ultimately I was unsure what, if anything, I might learn from interviewing men on these topics specifically. To this end, I developed a preliminary interview guide, acquired approval from my Institutional Review Board, and built the pilot study into a course I would be teaching where, as part of the normal content of the course, students would learn to conduct interviews and do a basic interview study.[3] I decided, in this case, that my students would interview men of varied other social identities to learn what men said about various types of violence, about manhood itself, and about social movements like #MeToo. At the time, I did not know if I would pursue the study any further.

In the following spring semester, my students both expressed interest in doing this type of study and actively worked to do their own version of the study for class. As I did in the same course offering (Applied Sociology) every semester to that point, I trained them in in-depth interviewing, analysis of interview transcripts, and strategies for gaining respondents and building rapport.[4] After various types of practice with interviewing throughout the semester, my students selected respondents to interview for the project. At this point, I was curious about variations in how people who identified as men might react to the questions. Students were able to select any person who identified as a man, regardless of other demographic social locations. As a result, my students created a preliminary data set of 30 interviews with men of different races, sexualities, religious backgrounds, and sexes assigned at birth. Throughout the semester, I read the transcripts of these interviews as they arrived from my students and took notes on the similarities and differences in the responses of these 30 men.

Although there were subtle variations in the transcripts in relation to race, class, sex, sexual, and religious identities, I was primarily struck by how similar the transcripts were overall. I was further struck by the ways most of the men my students interviewed, regardless of other demographics, talked about protection in relation to manhood,[5] discussed the subjects related to violence in ways that implied approval or at least acceptance of violence in society,[6] and characterized #MeToo and other movements for women's rights in mostly negative ways. Thinking about these patterns in the interviews my students conducted, I began to wonder what an in-depth, systematic interview study of people who identify as men would reveal.[7] I also began to wonder what, if any, themes might emerge vis-à-vis manhood and topics related to violence among men who were able to achieve, at least theoretically, the hegemonic ideal in our nation. Finally, I began to wonder what, if anything, would change if I intentionally compared religious and non-religious men, if I asked about other minority movements that are not immediately associated with women, and if I dressed up as much as I could as a "man" for the interviews (most of my students presented as women or feminine for their interviews).[8]

With these questions percolating in my mind, I began to prepare to do the study at the heart of this book in the late spring of 2018. Working within the established contours of the Institutional Review Board approval I had acquired for the study, I began disseminating flyers through student networks and in the broader local community, searching for people who identified as men and would be interested in talking about their identities as men, social and political issues in the United States today, and thoughts about violence in society. As was the case for my students in their class project and preliminary interviews, it was not hard to find many men who were interested in talking about these subjects. As a result, I was able to be selective in my sampling for the project, which allowed me to specifically design the contours and sample of the study throughout the data collection period.

SAMPLING

As suggested above, the project itself was designed in an inductive manner.[9] As I read through the preliminary interview transcripts, I took notes on questions that seemed most salient to the men my students interviewed and on issues within the transcripts where I could expect to do more or less probing to gain rich detail from the interviewees. At the same time, I planned from the start to only interview men who also identified as white, middle- or upper-class, with at least some college to date, between the ages of 18 and 24, cisgender, and heterosexual.[10] I would begin each interview with these basic questions, and when a given respondent did not fit one or more of these characteristics, I thanked them for their time and moved on to the next interview. However, since I was curious about potential differences between religious and non-religious men,[11] I intentionally split the interview sample in half between these two groups in hopes of learning what, if any, difference religion might make in men's responses to issues related to violence in society.

As a result, I constructed a sample of 50 people who identified as cisgender, heterosexual, white, middle- and upper-class men between the ages of 18 and 24. The sample also included 25 people who identified as religious in varied ways and 25 people who identified as non-religious in varied ways. All of the people I interviewed had some college at that point in their lives, and each one was living in the Central Florida area at the time. Although it did not create any significant variation in the interviews, 10 of the interviewees identified themselves as feminists, and the interview sample was split fairly equitably between those who identified as liberal (15), moderate (21), and conservative (14) politically.

Likely as a result of the characteristics of the Central Florida region (e.g., tourism, migration, heavy concentration of colleges and universities), most of the interviewees were originally from other parts of the country (38) though 12 of them were from Florida, and 10 more were from other states in the southeastern United States. The other 28 were from the northeast (11), midwest (10), and western (7) regions of the United States, but I did not see any significant variation in their responses by region. However, this might have been different if I had been asking about regional issues and politics instead of issues and political debates occurring throughout the United States today. In fact, I suggest regionally specific—as well as political identification specific—studies of this sort might make interesting contributions to my work here.

INTERVIEW DESIGN AND PERFORMANCE

With the design of the sample in mind, the interviews proceeded in an open-ended, conversational fashion.[12] I conducted each of the interviews in either my office at the University of Tampa or in a public place chosen by the respondent. The interviews lasted between one and a half and three hours in length, but the average interview was about one hour and forty-five minutes long. Rather than a structured question-and-answer protocol, I utilized a conversational[13] format wherein the respondent was asked about a topic (e.g., "What do you think about domestic violence?") and then given full latitude to talk as much or as little as they wanted to about the subject. As the interviewee spoke, I probed them with follow-up questions to steer the conversation when necessary (e.g., "And what do you mean by that?" or "Could you give me an example of that?").[14] The interviews were transcribed verbatim, and these transcriptions provided the raw data for this study and the quotes shared throughout this book.

Since the interview consisted of topical opportunities rather than structured questions, many topics came up in passing from the interviewees themselves. These topics included video games and other media, sports of various types, celebrities, and political figures. Further, since researchers have suggested doing so when interviewing men,[15] I dressed as masculine as possible, grew and then wore a beard throughout the data collection period, and presented my body language in as stereotypically masculine fashion as possible. I also spoke with interviewees in a deferential manner and regularly suggested that I was hoping I could learn from them about things I might not understand as well as they did. In this way, I played into their own masculine identities, as other interviewers have suggested, to increase their sense of comfort and control throughout the process. As such, I sought to create a situation where they felt free to discuss "manly" perspectives on society, gender, and violence throughout the interviews.

Although the shape and form of specific questions varied in relation to the reactions of the interviewees throughout the interviews, the following topics were covered in each of the interviews and were typically worded in an open-ended manner (e.g., what do you think about . . . or what does it mean to be . . .):

1. How would you describe your:

   a. Race
   b. Class
   c. Gender
   d. Sexuality
   e. Age
   f. Worldview in terms of religion or non-religion

2. What does it mean to be . . .

   a. A man
   b. Heterosexual
   c. White
   d. Middle or upper class (depending on interviewee)

3. How do you know you are a man? How do others know this about you?
4. What is the difference between being a man and being a woman?
5. What do you think about:

   a. Relations between men and women in America
   b. Abortion
   c. Women in the workplace
   d. The #MeToo movement

      i. Other minority movements like Black Lives Matter or same-sex marriage movements

   e. LGBT populations

      i. Lesbian and bisexual women
      ii. People who are female that don't identify as women
      iii. Transgender women
      iv. Gay men, bisexual men, transgender men
      v. Asexual women and men
      vi. Non-binary people

   f. Violence

      i. Probe for types they might mention or think about

   g. Guns

      i. Gun control
      ii. Gun debates
      iii. Mass shootings

    h. Sexual abuse

       i. Domestic violence
       ii. Harassment
       iii. Rape
       iv. Sexual assault

    i. Other types of violence in society
    j. What does the word *feminism* mean to you?
    k. What else would you like to share?

Since I gave respondents full latitude on how much or how little they said, it is not surprising that some topics held much more interest for them than others.[16] While I probed on every topic, there were certain aspects that received more or less discussion in specific interviews. The topics of focus in this book, however, represent topics where almost all the men had much to say with a couple of notable exceptions mentioned in the previous chapters.[17] Rather than deciding ahead of time what the focus of the analysis would be, I followed the respondents' own decision making regarding what topics were most salient to them.[18]

DATA ANALYSIS

As a sociological researcher who has published qualitative and quantitative research throughout the past decade,[19] I approached the interview transcripts here in an inductive manner.[20] I wasn't sure what they would hold, and therefore, I let the transcripts (i.e., the words the men shared in the interviews) speak for themselves. To this end, I began by reading through the entire set of transcripts in a close, line-by-line manner while taking notes on themes and recurring patterns in the statements made by the interviewees. In so doing, I developed a rough outline of what seemed like the most common and most salient topics in the data. With this in mind, I went back through the data set four times to verify that these were the most common and salient topics. Once this outline was complete, I began to focus on these topics throughout the next round of reading, reviewing, and organizing the transcripts.

    This next round consisted of focused selection of each situation wherein respondents discussed a given topic (e.g., whiteness or domestic violence). Each of these quotes were put into a file labeled with the topic (e.g., whiteness examples) and identified with a pseudonym as well as the age and (non)religious identity of the respondent. In this way, I created files full of quotes that discussed the same topic, and these files became the focus of my data analysis. Stated in a simple manner, each file consisted of each example where a given topic was discussed by a given respondent (or by the same respondent multiple times throughout the interview). In this way, the initial collection of transcriptions organized by interviewee became a collection of files organized by the topic and theme of the quotes within each file.

With these files in hand, I began to search each file for three things. I completed this same process with each of the thematic files. First, I outlined the similarities and differences in the ways each of the quotes discussed the topic at hand. I did this to gain an idea of the overall statement the men, as a group, were making on any given topic. Then, I pulled out quotes that were representative of each collected set of quotes. This provided examples I could use to illustrate the broader theme, as I did throughout this book. Although I sought to use the most representative quotes in each case, I also intentionally made sure to include at least one quote by each respondent among the quotes presented in this book. Finally, I wrote detailed memos and notes to explain, discuss, and characterize the overall themes, similarities and differences, and other aspects of the quotes in each file. These memos and notes provided the rough drafts of the analysis throughout this book.

As data analysis continued, I was granted the opportunity to present portions of this work at other universities and academic conferences. In such cases, I chose one of the thematic files (e.g., men's responses to gun violence) and composed a speech and illustration of this thematic content. I practiced both how to deliver and discuss the themes in the data in front of an audience of colleagues and gathered feedback concerning, for example, clarity, potential literatures to explore, and other prospective improvements to the work over time. In so doing, I was able to practice and revise the contents of the analyses in this book at different places and in front of different audiences as I composed the varied drafts of the book presented here. This process allowed me to both continuously refine the thematic points and implications of each chapter and incorporate insights and thoughts I might not have considered that were important or implicated in my presentations for other scholars with different standpoints and backgrounds.

The combination of these processes continued throughout the process of formulating, proposing, writing, and revising this book. Specifically, I sought to continuously analyze and revise the works presented here in hopes of capturing both the fullest portrait of what I learned about manhood and violence from the men I interviewed and the clearest method whereby I could translate these lessons and their implications for society to others of varied backgrounds, perspectives, and epistemological traditions. I also continuously sought feedback on in-progress drafts of the chapters from colleagues who study gender, masculinities, and/or violence. Through this ongoing iterative process, the contents of this book came to light in stages and were refined in many ways to capture the themes in the data as well as the ways such data could speak to others studying or otherwise concerned about relationships between manhood and violence in contemporary U.S. society.

NOTES

1. See note 1 in chapter 6.
2. Leavy, *Method Meets Art*; Leavy and Harris, *Contemporary Feminist Research.*
3. Syllabi and other information on the course available upon request.
4. This is on top of other training in these areas they receive in Research Methods and/or Qualitative Research Methods courses within our program.
5. See also Connell, *Gender and Power.*
6. See also Martin, *Rape Work.*
7. See Kleinman, *Feminist Fieldwork Analysis.*
8. Schwalbe and Wolkomir, "The Masculine Self as Problem and Resource."
9. See Berg and Lune, *Qualitative Research Methods*; Charmaz, *Constructing Grounded Theory*; and Kleinman, *Feminist Fieldwork Analysis* for qualitative inductive methods.
10. See Connell and Messerschmidt, "Hegemonic Masculinity."
11. See Goffman, "The Arrangement between the Sexes."
12. Berg and Lune, *Qualitative Methods*; Charmaz, *Constructing Grounded Theory*; Kleinman, *Feminist Fieldwork Analysis*; Leavy, *Method Meets Art.*
13. See Charmaz, *Constructing Grounded Theory.*
14. See Leavy, *Method Meets Art.*
15. McQueeney, "Doing Ethnography in a Sexist World"; Schrock and Koontz Anthony, "Diversifying Feminist Ethnographers' Dilemmas"; Schwalbe and Wolkomir, "The Masculine Self."
16. Charmaz, *Constructing Grounded Theory*; Leavy, *Method Meets Art.*
17. See the discussion on the #MeToo movement in chapter 6 for examples.
18. Charmaz, *Constructing Grounded Theory.*
19. See www.jsumerau.com for examples.
20. Kleinman, *Feminist Fieldwork Analysis*; McQueeney, "Doing Ethnography."

Bibliography

Abelson, Miriam J. *Men in Place: Trans Masculinity, Race, and Sexuality in America*. Minneapolis: University of Minnesota Press, 2019.

Acker, Joan. "Inequality Regimes: Gender, Class, and Race in Organizations." *Gender & Society* 20, no. 4 (August 2006): 441–64.

Acosta, Katie L. "Cultivating a *Lesbiana Seria* Identity." *Sexualities* 19, no. 5–6 (September 2016): 517–34.

Acosta, Katie L. "Pulse: A Space for Resilience, a Home for the Brave." *QED: A Journal in GLBTQ Worldmaking* 3, no. 3 (Fall 2016): 107–10.

Adams, Tony E. *Narrating the Closet: An Autoethnography of Same-Sex Attraction*. Walnut Creek, CA: Left Coast Press, 2011.

Akihiko, Hirose, and Kay Kei-ho Pih. "Men Who Strike and Men Who Submit: Hegemonic and Marginalized Masculinities in Mixed Martial Arts." *Men and Masculinities* 13, no. 2 (December 2010): 190–209.

Alexander, Michelle. *The New Jim Crow: Mass Incarceration in the Age of Colorblindness*. New York: The New Press, 2010.

Anderson, Elijah. *Code of the Street: Decency, Violence, and the Moral Life of the Inner City*. New York: W.W. Norton & Co., 1999.

Asencio, Marysol. "'Locas,' Respect, and Masculinity: Gender Conformity in Migrant Puerto Rican Gay Masculinities." *Gender & Society* 25, no. 3 (June 2011): 335–54.

Aune, Kristin. "Fatherhood in British Evangelical Christianity: Negotiating with Mainstream Culture." *Men and Masculinities* 13, no. 2 (December 2010): 168–89.

Avishai, Orit. "'Doing Religion' in a Secular World: Women in Conservative Religions and the Question of Agency." *Gender & Society* 22, no. 4 (August 2008): 409–33.

Barbee, Harry, and Douglas Schrock. "Un/gendering Social Selves: How Nonbinary People Navigate and Experience a Binarily Gendered World." *Sociological Forum* 34, no. 3 (September 2019): 572–93.

Barber, Kristen. "'Men Wanted': Heterosexual Aesthetic Labor in the Masculinization of the Hair Salon." *Gender & Society* 30, no. 4 (August 2016): 618–42.

Barber, Kristen, and Tristan Bridges. "Marketing Manhood in a 'Post-Feminist' Age." *Contexts* 16, no. 2 (2017): 38–43.

Barringer, M. N., David A. Gay, and John P. Lynxwiler. "Gender, Religiosity, Spirituality, and Attitudes toward Homosexuality." *Sociological Spectrum* 33, no. 3 (2013): 240–57.

Becker, Sarah, and Jill A. McCorkel. "The Gender of Criminal Opportunity: The Impact of Male Co-Offenders on Women's Crime." *Feminist Criminology* 6, no. 2 (April 2011): 79–110.

Bedera, Nicole, and Kristjane Nordmeyer. "An Inherently Masculine Practice: Understanding the Sexual Victimization of Queer Women." *Journal of Interpersonal Violence* (January 2020). https://doi.org/10.1177/0886260519898439.

Bedera, Nicole, and Kristjane Nordmeyer. "Never Go Out Alone: An Analysis of College Rape Prevention Tips." *Sexuality & Culture* 19, no. 3 (Winter 2015): 533–42.

Beemyn, Genny, and Susan Rankin. *The Lives of Transgender People.* New York: Columbia University Press, 2011.

Bellwether, Mira. *Fucking Trans Women.* October 2010.

Berg, Bruce L., and Howard Lune. *Qualitative Research Methods for the Social Sciences.* 8th ed. Essex, UK: Pearson, 2014.

Berg, Mark T. "Trends in the Lethality of American Violence." *Homicide Studies* 23, no. 3 (August 2019): 262–84.

Berger, Peter L., and Thomas Luckmann. *The Social Construction of Reality: A Treatise in the Sociology of Knowledge.* New York: Doubleday, 1966.

Bergstrand, Kelly, and James M. Jasper. "Villains, Victims, and Heroes in Character Theory and Affect Control Theory." *Social Psychology Quarterly* 81, no. 3 (September 2018): 228–47.

Besen-Cassino, Yasemin. "Gender Threat and Men in the Post-Trump World: The Effects of a Changing Economy on Men's Housework." *Men and Masculinities* 22, no. 1 (April 2019): 44–52.

Blumer, Herbert. *Symbolic Interaction: Perspective and Method.* Los Angeles: University of California Press, 1969.

Boag, Peter. *Same-Sex Affairs: Constructing and Controlling Homosexuality in the Pacific Northwest.* Los Angeles: University of California Press, 2003.

Bonilla-Silva, Eduardo. *Racism without Racists: Colorblind Racism and the Persistence of Racial Inequality in the United States.* Lanham, MD: Rowman & Littlefield, 2003.

Bor, J., A. S. Venkataramani, D. R. Williams, and A. C. Tsai. "Police Killings and Their Spillover Effects on the Mental Health of Black Americans: A Population-Based Quasi-Experimental Study." *Lancet* 392, no. 10144 (2018): 253–358.

Boyle, Kaitlin M. "Sexual Assault and Identity Disruption: A Sociological Approach to Posttraumatic Stress." *Society and Mental Health* 7, no. 2 (July 2017): 69–84.

Boyle, Kaitlin M. "Social Psychological Processes That Facilitate Sexual Assault within the Fraternity Party Subculture." *Sociology Compass* 9, no. 5 (May 2015): 386–99.

Boyle, Kaitlin M., and Lisa Slattery Walker. "The Neutralization and Denial of Sexual Violence in College Party Subcultures." *Deviant Behavior* 37, no. 12 (2016): 1392–410.

Branch, Kathryn, Carly M. Hilinski-Rosick, Emily Johnson, and Gabriela Solano. "Revenge Porn Victimization of College Students in the United States: An Exploratory Analysis." *International Journal of Cyber Criminology* 11, no. 1 (June 2017): 128–42.

Branch, Kathryn A., and Tara N. Richards. "The Effects of Receiving a Rape Disclosure: College Friends' Stories." *Violence Against Women* 19, no. 5 (May 2013): 658–70.

Bridges, Tristan. "The Costs of Exclusionary Practices in Masculinities Studies." *Men and Masculinities* 22, no. 1 (April 2019): 16–33.

Bridges, Tristan. "A Very 'Gay' Straight? Hybrid Masculinities, Sexual Aesthetics, and the Changing Relationship between Masculinity and Homophobia." *Gender & Society* 28, no. 1 (February 2014): 58–82.

Bridges, Tristan, and C. J. Pascoe. "Hybrid Masculinities: New Directions in the 2014 Sociology of Men and Masculinities." *Sociology Compass* 8, no. 3 (March 2014): 426–58.

Browne, Angela, and Kirk R. Williams. "Gender, Intimacy, and Lethal Violence: Trends from 1976 through 1987." *Gender & Society* 7, no. 1 (March 1993): 78–98.

Buggs, Shantel Gabrieal. "Color, Culture, or Cousin? Multiracial Americans and Framing Boundaries in Interracial Relationships." *Journal of Marriage and Family* 81, no. 5 (October 2019): 1221–36.

Buggs, Shantel Gabrieal. "Dating in the Time of #BlackLivesMatter: Mixed Race Women's Discourses of Race and Racism." *Sociology of Race and Ethnicity* 3, no. 4 (October 2017): 538–51.

Buggs, Shantel Gabrieal. "(Dis)Owning Exotic: Navigating Race, Intimacy, and Trans Identity." *Sociological Inquiry* 90, no. 2 (May 2020): 249–70.

Buggs, Shantel Gabrieal. "Does (Mixed-)Race Matter? The Role of Race in Interracial Sex, Dating, and Marriage." *Sociology Compass* 11, no. 11 (November 2017): 1–13.

Burke, Kelsy. *Christians under Covers: Evangelicals and Sexual Pleasure on the Internet.* Oakland: University of California Press, 2016.

Butler, Judith. *Gender Trouble: Feminism and the Subversion of Identity.* New York: Routledge, 1999.

Calasanti, Toni M., and Kathleen F. Slevin. *Gender, Social Inequalities, and Aging.* Walnut Creek, CA: Altamira Press, 2001.

Califia, Pat. *Sex Changes: Transgender Politics.* Jersey City, NJ: Cleis Press, 2012.

Canan, Sasha N., Kristen N. Jozkowski, Jacquelyn Wiersma-Mosley, Heather Blunt-Vinti, and Mindy Bradley. "Validation of the Sexual Experience Survey: Short Form Revised Using Lesbian, Bisexual, and Heterosexual Women's Narratives of Sexual Violence." *Archives of Sexual Behavior* 49, no. 3 (2020): 1067–83.

Carlson, Jennifer. *Citizen-Protectors: The Everyday Politics of Guns in an Age of Decline.* New York: Oxford University Press, 2015.

Carlson, Jennifer. "Legally Armed but Presumed Dangerous: An Intersectional Analysis of Gun Carry Licensing as a Racial/Gender Degradation Ceremony." *Gender & Society* 32, no. 2 (April 2018): 204–27.

Carlson, Jennifer. "Mourning Mayberry: Guns, Masculinity, and Socioeconomic Decline." *Gender & Society* 29, no. 3 (June 2015): 386–409.

Carlson, Jennifer. "Revisiting the Weberian Presumption: Gun Militarism, Gun Populism and the Racial Politics of Legitimate Violence in Policing." *American Journal of Sociology* 125, no. 3 (November 2019): 633–82.

Carrigan, Tim, Raewyn Connell, and John Lee. 1985. "Toward a New Sociology of Masculinity." *Theory and Society* 14, no. 5 (September): 551–604.

Carruthers, Charlene A. *Unapologetic: A Black, Queer, and Feminist Mandate for Radical Movements.* Boston: Beacon Press, 2018.

Castañeda, Claudia. "Developing Gender: The Medical Treatment of Transgender Young People." *Social Science & Medicine* 143 (October 2015): 262–70.

Charmaz, Kathy. *Constructing Grounded Theory: A Practical Guide through Qualitative Analysis.* Thousand Oaks, CA: Sage, 2006.

Cheng, Cliff. "Marginalized Masculinities and Hegemonic Masculinity: An Introduction." *Journal of Men's Studies* 7, no. 3 (June 1999): 295–315.

Cimino, Richard, and Christopher Smith. *Atheist Awakening: Secular Activism and Community in America.* New York: Oxford, 2014.

Cimino, Richard, and Christopher Smith. "Secular Humanism and Atheism beyond Progressive Secularism." *Sociology of Religion* 68, no. 4 (2007): 407–24.

Codrea-Rado, Anna. "#MeToo Floods Social Media with Stories of Harassment and Assault." *New York Times*, October 16, 2017. https://www.nytimes.com/2017/10/16/technology/metoo-twitter-facebook.html.

Coley, Jonathan S. *Gay on God's Campus: Mobilizing for LGBT Equality at Christian Colleges and Universities.* Chapel Hill: University of North Carolina Press, 2018.

Collins, Patricia Hill. *Black Feminist Thought: Knowledge, Consciousness, and the Politics of Empowerment.* 2nd ed. New York: Routledge, 2000.

Collins, Patricia Hill. *Black Sexual Politics: African Americans, Gender, and the New Racism.* New York: Routledge, 2004.

Collins, Patricia Hill. *Intersectionality as Critical Social Theory.* Durham, NC: Duke University Press, 2019.

Combahee River Collective. "A Black Feminist Statement." Reprinted in *The Second Wave: A Reader in Feminist Theory.* New York: Routledge, 1997 [1977].

Connell, Catherine. "Doing, Undoing, or Redoing Gender? Learning from the Workplace Experiences of Transpeople." *Gender & Society* 24, no. 1 (February 2010): 31–55.

Connell, Raewyn. "Accountable Conduct: 'Doing Gender' in Transsexual and Political Retrospect." *Gender & Society* 23, no. 1 (February 2009): 104–11.

Connell, Raewyn. *Gender and Power*. Stanford, CA: Stanford University Press, 1987.

Connell, Raewyn. *Masculinities*. Cambridge: Polity Press, 1995.

Connell, Raewyn. *The Men and the Boys*. Berkeley: University of California Press, 2001.

Connell, Raewyn, and James Messerschmidt. "Hegemonic Masculinity: Rethinking the Concept." *Gender & Society* 19, no. 6 (December 2005): 829–59.

Cooper, Brittney. *Eloquent Rage: A Black Feminist Discovers Her Superpower*. New York: St. Martin's Press, 2018.

Corzine, Jay, and Lin Huff-Corzine. "Racial Inequality and Black Homicide: An Analysis of Felony, Nonfelony, and Total Rates." *Journal of Contemporary Criminal Justice* 8, no. 2 (May 1992): 150–65.

Costello, Cary Gabriel. "Not a 'Medical Miracle': Intersex Reproduction and the Medical Enforcement of Binary Sex and Gender." In *Maternity and Motherhood: Narrative and Theoretical Perspectives on Queer Conception, Birth, and Parenting*, edited by Margaret F. Gibson, 63–80. Ontario: Demeter Press, 2014.

Costello, Cary Gabriel. "Trans and Intersex Children: Forced Sex Changes, Chemical Castration, and Self-Determination." In *Women's Health: Readings on Social, Economic, and Political Issues*. Dubuque, IA: Kendall Hunt, 2016.

Cottom, Tressie McMillan. *Lower Ed: The Troubling Rise of For-Profit Colleges in the New Economy*. New York: The New Press, 2017.

Cottom, Tressie McMillan. *Thick—and Other Essays*. New York: The New Press, 2019.

Courtenay, Will H. "Constructions of Masculinity and Their Influence on Men's Well-Being: A Theory of Gender and Health." *Social Science and Medicine* 50, no. 10 (June 2000): 1385–401.

Cragun, Ryan T., and J. E. Sumerau. "God May Save Your Life, but You Have to Find Your Own Keys: Religious Attributions and Religious Priming." *Archive for the Psychology of Religion* 37, no. 3 (December 2015): 321–42.

Cragun, Ryan T., and J. E. Sumerau. "The Last Bastion of Sexual and Gender Prejudice? Sexualities, Race, Gender, Religiosity, and Spirituality in the Examination of Prejudice toward Sexual and Gender Minorities." *Journal of Sex Research* 52, no. 7 (2015): 821–34.

Cragun, Ryan T., and J. E. Sumerau. "Losing Manhood Like a Man: A Collaborative Autoethnographic Examination of Masculinities and the Experience of a Vasectomy." *Men and Masculinities* 20, no. 1 (April 2017): 98–116.

Cragun, Ryan T., and J. E. Sumerau. "Men Who Hold More Egalitarian Attitudes toward Women Working outside the Home in the US: Who Are They?" *The Human Prospect: A Neohumanist Perspective* 4, no. 1 (2014): 10–24.

Cragun, Ryan T., and J. E. Sumerau. "No One Expects a Transgender Jew: Religious, Sexual, and Gendered Intersections in the Evaluation of Religious and Nonreligious Others." *Secularism and Nonreligion* 6, no. 1 (2017): 1–16. https://doi.org/10.5334/snr.82.

Creek, S. J. "'Not Getting Any Because of Jesus': The Centrality of Desire Management to the Identity Work of Gay, Celibate Christians." *Symbolic Interaction* 36, no. 2 (May 2013): 119–36.

Crenshaw, Kimberlé. "Mapping the Margins: Intersectionality, Identity Politics, and Violence against Women of Color." *Stanford Law Review* 46, no. 3 (July 1991): 1241–99.

Cromwell, Jason. *Transmen and FTMs: Identities, Bodies, Genders, and Sexualities*. Champaign: University of Illinois Press, 1999.

Cserni, Robert T., and Lee W. Essig. "Twenty Years of *Men and Masculinities* by the Numbers: An Analysis of Publications and Article Keywords." *Men and Masculinities* 22, no. 1 (April 2019): 5–15.

Currah, Paisley. "Expecting Bodies: The Pregnant Man and Transgender Exclusion from the Employment Non-Discrimination Act." *Women's Studies Quarterly* 36, no. 3–4 (December 2008): 330–36.

Darwin, Helana. "Doing Gender beyond the Binary: A Virtual Ethnography." *Symbolic Interaction* 40, no. 3 (August 2017): 317–34.

Davis, Georgiann. *Contesting Intersex: The Dubious Diagnosis*. New York: New York University Press, 2015.

Davis, Georgiann, Jodie M. Dewey, and Erin L. Murphy. "Giving Sex: Deconstructing Intersex and Trans Medicalization Practices." *Gender & Society* 30, no. 3 (June 2016): 490–514.

Davis, Heath Fogg. *Beyond Trans: Does Gender Matter?* New York: New York University Press, 2017.

Dellinger, Kristen. "Masculinities in 'Safe' and 'Embattled' Organizations: Accounting for Pornographic and Feminist Magazines." *Gender & Society* 18, no. 5 (October 2004): 545–66.

Dingwall, Robert. "Notes toward an Intellectual History of Symbolic Interactionism." *Symbolic Interaction* 24, no. 2 (2001): 237–42.

Doan, Petra. "To Count or Not to Count: Queering Measurement and the Transgender Community." *Women's Studies Quarterly* 44, no. 3–4 (Fall/Winter 2016): 89–110.

Doane, Ashley W., and Eduardo Bonilla-Silva (Eds.). *White Out: The Continuing Significance of Racism*. New York: Routledge, 2003.

Doering, Jan. "Face, Accounts, and Schemes in the Context of Relationship Breakups." *Symbolic Interaction* 33, no. 1 (Winter 2010): 71–95.

Dowd-Arrow, Benjamin, Terrence D. Hill, and Amy M. Burdette. "Gun Ownership and Fear." *SSM: Population Health* 8 (2019): 1–7.

Dozier, Raine. "Beards, Breasts, and Bodies: Doing Sex in a Gendered World." *Gender & Society* 19, no. 3 (June 2005): 297–316.

Driskill, Qwo-Li, Daniel Heath Justice, Deborah Miranda, and Lisa Tatonetti (Eds.). *Sovereign Erotics: A Collection of Two-Spirit Literature*. Tuscon: University of Arizona Press, 2011.

Duggan, Lisa. *The Twilight of Equality? Neoliberalism, Cultural Politics and the Attack on Democracy*. Boston: Beacon Press, 2004.

Dunn, Jennifer Leigh, and S. J. Creek. "Identity Dilemmas: Toward a More Situated Understanding." *Symbolic Interaction* 38, no. 2 (May 2015): 261–84.

Eastman, Jason T., and Douglas P. Schrock. "Southern Rock Musicians' Construction of White Trash." *Race, Gender & Class* 15, no. 1–2 (2008): 205–19.

Eisner, Shiri. *Bi: Notes for a Bisexual Revolution*. Berkeley, CA: Seal Press, 2013.

Ekşi, Betül. "Police and Masculinities in Transition in Turkey: From Macho to Reformed to Militarized Policing." *Men and Masculinities* 22, no. 3 (August 2019): 491–515.

Emig, Rainer. "Terrorist Masculinities: Political Masculinity between Fiction, Facts, and Their Mediation." *Men and Masculinities* 22, no. 3 (August 2019): 516–28.

Espiritu, Y. L. "'We Don't Sleep Around Like White Girls Do': Family, Culture and Gender in Filipina American Lives." *Signs* 26, no. 2 (2001): 415–40.

Evans, Lorraine, and Kimberly Davies. "No Sissy Boys Here: A Content Analysis of the Representation of Masculinity in Elementary School Reading Textbooks." *Sex Roles* 42 (February 2000): 255–70.

Ezzell, Matthew B. "Barbie Dolls on the Pitch: Identity Work, Defensive Othering, and Inequality in Women's Rugby." *Social Problems* 56, no. 1 (February 2009): 111–31.

Ezzell, Matthew B. "'I'm in Control': Compensatory Manhood Acts in a Therapeutic Community." *Gender & Society* 26, no. 2 (April 2012): 190–215.

Ezzell, Matthew B. "Pornography, Lad Mags, Video Games, and Boys: Reviving the Canary in the Cultural Coal Mine." In *The Sexualization of Childhood*, edited by Sharna Olfman, 7–32. Westport, CT: Praeger, 2009.

Fausto-Sterling, Anne. *Sexing the Body: Gender Politics and the Construction of Sexuality*. New York: Basic Books, 2000.

Feagin, Joe R. *The White Racial Frame: Centuries of Racial Framing and Counter-Framing*. New York: Routledge, 2010.

Feinberg, Leslie. *Stone Butch Blues: A Novel*. Old Chelsea Station, NY: Alyson Books, 1993.

Fenstermaker, Sarah. "The Turn from 'What' to 'How': Garfinkel's Reach beyond Description." *Symbolic Interaction* 39, no. 2 (May 2016): 295–305.

Ferguson, Ann Arnett. *Bad Boys: Public Schools in the Making of Black Masculinity*. Ann Arbor: University of Michigan Press, 2000.

Ferguson, Roderick. *Aberrations in Black: Toward a Queer of Color Critique*. Minneapolis: University of Minnesota Press, 2004.

Fetner, Tina. *How the Religious Right Shaped Lesbian and Gay Activism*. Minneapolis: University of Minnesota Press, 2008.

Fields, Jessica. "Normal Queers: Straight Parents Respond to Their Children's 'Coming Out.'" *Symbolic Interaction* 24, no. 2 (2001): 165–87.

Figueroa, Daniel. "Accused Seminole Heights Killer Was Arrested One Year Ago Today." *Tampa Bay Times*, November 28, 2018. https://www.tampabay.com/news/publicsafety/accused-seminole-heights-killer-was-arrested-one-year-ago-today-20181128/.

Foucault, Michel. *Discipline and Punish: The Birth of the Prison*. 2nd ed. New York: Vintage Books, 1995.

Foucault, Michel. *The History of Sexuality, Volume 1: An Introduction*. New York: Vintage Books, 1978.

Fox, James Alan, and Monica J. DeLateur. "Mass Shootings in America: Moving beyond Newton." *Homicide Studies* 18, no. 1 (February 2014): 125–45.

Fox, James Alan, and Jack Levin. "Multiple Homicide: Patterns of Serial and Mass Murder." *Crime and Justice* 23 (1998): 407–55.

Friedman, Jaclyn, and Jessica Valenti (Eds.). *Yes Means Yes! Visions of Female Sexual Power and a World without Rape*. Berkeley, CA: Seal Press, 2008.

Garcia, Lorena. *Respect Yourself, Protect Yourself: Latina Girls and Sexual Identity*. New York: New York University Press, 2012.

Garfinkel, Harold. *Studies in Ethnomethodology*. Malden, MA: Blackwell Publishers, 1967.

Garland, Tammy S., Kathryn A. Branch, and Mackenzie Grimes. "Blurring the Lines: Reinforcing Rape Myths in Comic Books." *Feminist Criminology* 11, no. 1 (January 2016): 48–68.

Garland, Tammy S., Christina Policastro, Kathryn A. Branch, and Brandy B. Henderson. "Bruised and Battered: Reinforcing Intimate Partner Violence in Comic Books." *Feminist Criminology* 14, no. 5 (December 2019): 584–611.

Garrison, Spencer. "On the Limits of 'Trans Enough': Authenticating Trans Identity Narratives." *Gender & Society* 32, no. 5 (October 2018): 613–37.

Gay, Roxane. *Bad Feminist: Essays*. New York: Harper, 2014.

Gay, Roxane (Ed.). *Not That Bad: Dispatches from Rape Culture*. New York: Harper, 2018.

Gerber, Lynne. "Grit, Guts, and Vanilla Beans: Godly Masculinity in the Ex-Gay Movement." *Gender & Society* 29, no. 1 (February 2015): 26–50.

Gilbert, Sophie. "The Movement of #MeToo: How a Hashtag Got Its Power." *The Atlantic*, October 16, 2017. https://www.theatlantic.com/entertainment/archive/2017/10/the-movement-of-metoo/542979/.

Goffman, Erving. "The Arrangement between the Sexes." *Theory and Society* 4, no. 3 (Autumn 1977): 301–31.

Goffman, Erving. *Frame Analysis: An Essay on the Organization of Experience*. New York: Harper & Row, 1974.

Goffman, Erving. *Interaction Ritual: Essays on Face-to-Face Interaction*. Oxford: Aldine, 1967.

Goffman, Erving. *The Presentation of Self in Everyday Life*. New York: Anchor Books, 1959.

Goffman, Erving. *Stigma: Notes on the Management of Spoiled Identity*. New York: Simon & Schuster, 1963.

Gossett, Jennifer Lynn, and Sarah Byrne. "'Click Here': A Content Analysis of Internet Rape Sites." *Gender & Society* 16, no. 5 (October 2002): 689–709.

Grace, Laura Jane, and Dan Ozzi. *Tranny: Confessions of Punk Rock's Most Infamous Anarchist Sellout*. New York: Hachette Books, 2016.

Halberstam, J. *In a Queer Time and Place: Transgender Bodies, Subcultural Lives*. New York: New York University Press, 2005.

Hale, C. "Fear of Crime: A Review of the Literature." *International Review of Victimology* 4, no. 2 (January 1996): 79–150.

Hamilton, Laura. "Trading on Heterosexuality: College Women's Gender Strategies and Homophobia." *Gender & Society* 21, no. 2 (April 2007): 145–72.

Harder, Brittany M., and J. E. Sumerau. "Understanding Gender as a Fundamental Cause of Health: Simultaneous Linear Relationships between Gender, Mental Health, and Physical Health over Time." *Sociological Spectrum* 38, no. 6 (2019): 387–405.

Hassan, Naeemul, Manash Kumar Mandal, Mansurul Bhuiyan, Aparna Moitra, and Syed Ishtiague Ahmed. "Nonparticipation of Bangladeshi Women in #MeToo Movement." *Proceedings of the Tenth International Conference on Information and Communication Technologies and Development*, no. 29, 2019.

Heath, Melanie. *One Marriage under God: The Campaign to Promote Marriage in America.* New York: New York University Press, 2012.

Hill, Terrence D., Benjamin Dowd-Arrow, Andrew P. Davis, and Amy M. Burdette. "Happiness Is a Warm Gun? Gun Ownership and Happiness in the United States (1973–2018)." *SSM: Population Health* 10 (2020): 1–6.

Hlavka, Heather R. "Normalizing Sexual Violence: Young Women Account for Harassment and Abuse." *Gender & Society* 28, no. 3 (June 2014): 337–58.

Holland, Kathryn, and Nicole Bedera. "'Call for Help Immediately': A Discourse Analysis of Resident Assistants' Responses to Sexual Assault Disclosures." *Violence Against Women* (July 2019). https://doi.org/10.1177/1077801219863879.

Hollander, Jocelyn. "'I Demand More of People': Accountability, Interaction, and Gender Change." *Gender & Society* 27, no. 1 (2013): 5–29.

Hollander, Jocelyn, and C. J. Pascoe. "Comment on Brush and Miller's 'Trouble in Paradigm': Gender Transformative Programming in Violence Prevention." *Violence Against Women* 25, no. 14 (November 2019): 1682–88.

Huff-Corzine, Lin, James C. McCutcheon, Jay Corzine, John P. Jarvis, Melissa J. Tetzlaff-Bemiller, Mindy Weller, and Matt Landon. "Shooting for Accuracy: Comparing Data Sources on Mass Murder." *Homicide Studies* 18, no. 1 (February 2014): 105–24.

Huff-Corzine, Lin, Sarah Ann Sacra, Jay Corzine, and Rachel Rados. "Florida's Task Force Approach to Combat Human Trafficking: An Analysis of County-Level Data." *Police Practice and Research* 18, no. 2 (2017): 1–14.

Jackson, Brandon A., and Adia Harvey Wingfield. "Getting Angry to Get Ahead: Black College Men, Emotional Performance, and Encouraging Respectable Masculinity." *Symbolic Interaction* 36, no. 3 (August 2013): 275–92.

James, S. E., J. L. Herman, S. Rankin, M. Keisling, L. Mottet, and M. Anafi. *The Report of the 2015 U.S. Transgender Survey.* Washington, DC: National Center for Transgender Equality, 2016.

Jauk, Daniela. "Gender Violence Revisited: Lessons from Violent Victimization of Transgender Identified Individuals." *Sexualities* 16, no. 7 (2013): 807–25.

Johnson, Allan G. *The Gender Knot: Unraveling Our Patriarchal Legacy.* Philadelphia: Temple University Press, 2014.

Johnson, Austin H. "Normative Accountability: How the Medical Model Influences Transgender Identities and Experiences." *Sociology Compass* 9, no. 9 (2015): 803–13.

Johnson, Austin H. "Transnormativity: A New Concept and Its Validation through Documentary Film about Transgender Men." *Sociological Inquiry* 86, no. 4 (November 2016): 465–91.

Jones, Angela. "The Pleasures of Fetishization: BBW Erotic Webcam Performers, Empowerment, and Pleasure." *Fat Studies* 8, no. 3 (2019): 279–98.

Kallivayalil, Diya. "Narratives of Suffering of South Asian Immigrant Survivors of Domestic Violence." *Violence Against Women* 16, no. 7 (July 2010): 789–811.

Karkazis, Katrina. *Fixing Sex: Intersex, Medical Authority, and Lived Experience.* Durham, NC: Duke University Press, 2008.

Kasim, Muhammadali P. "Mappila Muslim Masculinities: A History of Contemporary Abjectification." *Men and Masculinities* (2018). DOI: 10.1177/1097184X18803658.

Katz, Jack. "Essences as Moral Identities: Verifiability and Responsibility in Imputations of Deviance and Charisma." *American Journal of Sociology* 80, no. 6 (1975): 1369–90.

Katz, Jonathan Ned. *The Invention of Heterosexuality.* Chicago: University of Chicago Press, 1995.

Kelley, Kristin, and Jeff Gruenewald. "Accomplishing Masculinity through Anti-Lesbian, Gay, Bisexual, and Transgender Homicide: A Comparative Case Study Approach." *Men and Masculinities* 18, no. 1 (April 2015): 3–29.

Khan-Cullors, Patrisse, and asha bandele. *When They Call You a Terrorist: A Black Lives Matter Memoir*. New York: St. Martin's Press, 2018.

Khomani, Nadia. "#MeToo: How a Hashtag Became a Rallying Cry against Sexual Harassment." *Guardian*, October 20, 2017. https://www.theguardian.com/world/2017/oct/20/women-worldwide-use-hashtag-metoo-against-sexual-harassment.

Kleinman, Sherryl. *Feminist Fieldwork Analysis*. Thousand Oaks, CA: Sage, 2007.

Kleinman, Sherryl. *Opposing Ambitions: Gender and Identity in an Alternative Organization*. Chicago: University of Chicago Press, 1996.

Kolysh, S. "Straight Gods, White Devils: Exploring Paths to Non-Religion in the Lives of Black LGBTQ People." *Secularism and Nonreligion* 6, no. 2 (2017): 1–13.

Kong, Travis S. K. "Be a Responsible and Respectable Man: Two Generations of Chinese Gay Men Accomplishing Masculinity in Hong Kong." *Men and Masculinities* (2019). DOI: 10.1177/1097184X19859390.

Lageson, Sarah Esther, Suzy McElrath, and Krissinda Ellen Palmer. "Gendered Public Support for Criminalizing 'Revenge Porn.'" *Feminist Criminology* 14, no. 5 (December 2019): 560–83.

Lampe, Nik M., Shannon K. Carter, and J. E. Sumerau. "Continuity and Change in Gender Frames: The Case of Transgender Reproduction." *Gender & Society* (2019). DOI: 10.1177/0891243219857979.

Lampe, Nik, Lin Huff-Corzine, and Jay Corzine. "The Pulse Scrolls." *Homicide on the Rise: The Resurgence of Homicide in Urban America?* Proceedings of the 2018 Annual Meeting of the Homicide Research Working Group, Clearwater Beach, Florida.

Lanier, Christina, and Lin Huff-Corzine. "American Indian Homicide: A County Level Analysis Using Social Disorganization Theory." *Homicide Studies* 10, no. 3 (August 2006): 181–94.

Leavy, Patricia. *Method Meets Art: Arts-Based Research Practice*. 2nd ed. New York: Guilford Press, 2015.

Leavy, Patricia, and Anne Harris. *Contemporary Feminist Research from Theory to Practice*. New York: Guilford Press, 2019.

LeDrew, Stephen. "Discovering Atheism: Heterogeneity in Trajectories to Atheist Identity and Activism." *Sociology of Religion* 74, no. 4 (2013): 431–53.

Lee, Jooyoung. *Blowin' Up: Rap Dreams in South Central*. Chicago: University of Chicago Press, 2016.

Link, Bruce G., and Jo Phelan. "Social Conditions as Fundamental Causes of Disease." *Journal of Health and Social Behavior* (Extra Issue 1995): 80–94.

Linneman, Thomas J. "How Do You Solve a Problem Like Will Truman? The Feminization of Gay Masculinities on Will & Grace." *Men and Masculinities* 10, no. 5 (August 2008): 585–603.

Lombardi, Emilia. "Trans Issues in Sociology: A Trans-Centered Perspective." In *Other, Please Specify: Queer Methods in Sociology*, edited by D'Lane Compton, Tey Meadow, and Kristen Schilt, 67–79. Oakland: University of California Press, 2018.

Loseke, Donileen R. "The Study of Identity as Cultural, Institutional, Organizational, and Personal Narratives: Theoretical and Empirical Integrations." *Sociological Quarterly* 48, no. 4 (Fall 2007): 661–88.

Lubold, Amanda Marie. "Breastfeeding and Employment: A Propensity Score Matching Approach." *Sociological Spectrum* 36, no. 6 (2016): 391–405.

Lucal, Betsy. "What It Means to Be Gendered Me: Life on the Boundaries of a Dichotomous Gender System." *Gender & Society* 13, no. 6 (December 1999): 781–97.

MacLeod, Jay. *Ain't No Makin' It: Aspirations and Attainment in a Low-Income Neighborhood*. Boulder, CO: Westview Press.

Martin, Patricia Yancey. "Gender, Accounts, and Rape Processing Work." *Social Problems* 44, no. 4 (November 1997): 464–82.

Martin, Patricia Yancey. "Gender as a Social Institution." *Social Forces* 82, no. 4 (June 2004): 1249–73.

Martin, Patricia Yancey. "'Mobilizing Masculinities': Women's Experiences of Men at Work." *Organization* 8, no. 4 (November 2001): 587–618.

Martin, Patricia Yancey. *Rape Work: Victims, Gender, and Emotions in Organization and Community Context.* New York: Routledge, 2005.

Martin, Patricia Yancey. "'Said and Done' versus 'Saying and Doing': Gendering Practices, Practicing Gender at Work." *Gender & Society* 17, no. 3 (June 2003): 342–66.

Mathers, Lain A. B. "Bathrooms, Boundaries, and Emotional Burdens: Cisgendering Interactions through the Interpretation of Transgender Experience." *Symbolic Interaction* 40, no. 3 (August 2017): 295–316.

Mathers, Lain A. B. "Bi+ People's Experiences in the Post Gay Era." Unpublished dissertation, University of Illinois at Chicago, 2019.

Mathers, Lain A. B. "Expanding on the Experiences of Transgender Nonreligious People: An Exploratory Analysis." *Secularism and Nonreligion* 6 (2017): 1–10. https://doi.org/10.5334/snr.84.

Mathers, Lain A. B. "Navigating Genderqueer Existence within and beyond the Academy." In *Negotiating the Emotional Challenges of Conducting Deeply Personal Research in Health*, edited by Alexandra "Xan" C. H. Nowakowski and J. E. Sumerau, 125–34. New York: Routledge, 2017.

Mathers, Lain A. B., J. E. Sumerau, and Ryan T. Cragun. "The Limits of Homonormativity: Constructions of Bisexual and Transgender People in the Post-Gay Era." *Sociological Perspectives* 61, no. 6 (2018): 934–52.

Mathers, Lain A. B., J. E. Sumerau, and Koji Ueno. "'This Isn't Just Another Gay Group': Privileging Heterosexuality in a Mixed-Sexuality LGBTQ Advocacy Group." *Journal of Contemporary Ethnography* 47, no. 6 (December 2018): 834–64.

McCabe, Katharine, and J. E. Sumerau. "Reproductive Vocabularies: Interrogating Intersections of Reproduction, Sexualities, and Religion among U.S. Cisgender College Women." *Sex Roles* 78, no. 5–6 (March 2018): 352–66.

McCall, George, and J. L. Simmons. *Identities and Interactions: An Examination of Human Associations in Everyday Life.* New York: Free Press, 1966.

McDermott, Monica, and Frank L. Samson. "White Racial and Ethnic Identity in the United States." *Annual Review of Sociology* 31, no. 1 (August 2005): 245–61.

McDowell, Amy D. "Aggressive and Loving Men: Gender Hegemony in Christian Hardcore Punk." *Gender & Society* 31, no. 2 (April 2017): 223–44.

McGuire, Keon M., Jonathan Berhanu, Charles H. F. Davis, and Shaun R. Harper. "In Search of Progressive Black Masculinities: Critical Self-Reflections on Gender Identity Development among Black Undergraduate Men." *Men and Masculinities* 17, no. 3 (August 2014): 253–77.

McQueeney, Krista. "Doing Ethnography in a Sexist World: A Response to 'The Feminist Ethnographer's Dilemma.'" *Journal of Contemporary Ethnography* 42, no. 4 (August 2013): 451–59.

Meadow, Tey. *Trans Kids: Being Gendered in the Twenty-First Century.* Oakland: University of California Press, 2018.

Messerschmidt, James W. "Becoming 'Real Men': Adolescent Masculinity Challenges and Sexual Violence." *Men and Masculinities* 2, no. 3 (January 2000): 286–307.

Messerschmidt, James W. *Masculinities and Crime: A Quarter Century of Theory and Research.* Lanham, MD: Rowman & Littlefield, 2018.

Messner, Michael. "Boyhood, Organized Sports, and the Construction of Masculinities." *Journal of Contemporary Ethnography* 18, no. 4 (January 1990): 416–44.

Messner, Michael A. *Guys Like Me: Five Wars, Five Veterans for Peace.* New Brunswick, NJ: Rutgers University Press, 2018.

Messner, Michael A. *Out of Play: Critical Essays on Gender and Sport.* Albany, NY: State University of New York Press, 2007.

Messner, Michael A. *Power at Play: Sports and the Problem of Masculinity.* Boston: Beacon Press, 1992.

Metzl, Jonathan M. *Dying of Whiteness: How the Politics of Racial Resentment Is Killing America's Heartland*. New York: Basic Books, 2019.

Miller, Lisa R., and Eric Anthony Grollman. "The Social Costs of Gender Nonconformity for Transgender Adults: Implications for Discrimination and Health." *Sociological Forum* 30, no. 3 (September 2015): 809–31.

Mills, C. Wright. "Situated Actions and Vocabularies of Motive." *American Sociological Review* 5, no. 6 (December 1940): 904–13.

Mirandé, Alfredo, Juan M. Pitones, and Jesse Díaz Jr. "Quien Es el Mas Macho? A Comparison of Day Laborers and Chicano Men." *Men and Masculinities* 14, no. 3 (August 2011): 309–34.

Mock, Janet. *Redefining Realness: My Path to Womanhood, Identity, Love, and So Much More*. New York: Atria Paperback, 2014.

Moloney, Mairead Eastin, and Tony P. Love. "Assessing Online Misogyny: Perspectives from Sociology and Feminist Media Studies." *Sociology Compass* 12, no. 5 (May 2018): e12577.

Moon, Dawne. *God, Sex, and Politics: Homosexuality and Everyday Theologies*. Chicago: University of Chicago Press, 2004.

Moon, Dawne, Theresa W. Tobin, and J. E. Sumerau. "Alpha, Omega, and the Letters in Between: LGBTQI Conservative Christians Undoing Gender." *Gender & Society* 33, no. 4 (August 2019): 583–606.

Movement Advancement Project. "A Closer Look: Bisexual Transgender People." September 2017. http://www.lgbtmap.org/bisexual-transgender.

Mullaney, Jamie L. "Telling It Like a Man: Masculinities and Battering Men's Accounts of Their Violence." *Men and Masculinities* 10, no. 2 (October 2007): 222–47.

Navarro, Jordana N., and Jana L. Jasinski. "Going Cyber: Using Routine Activities Theory to Predict Cyberbullying Experiences." *Sociological Spectrum* 32, no. 1 (2012): 81–94.

Nowakowski, Alexandra C. H., and J. E. Sumerau. "Aging Partners Managing Chronic Illness Together: Introducing the Content Collection." *Gerontology and Geriatric Medicine* 3 (2017): 1–3.

Nowakowski, Alexandra "Xan" C. H., and J. E. Sumerau (Eds.). *Negotiating the Emotional Challenges of Conducting Deeply Personal Research in Health*. New York: Routledge, 2018.

Nowakowski, Alexandra C. H., and J. E. Sumerau. "Out of the Shadows: Partners Managing Illness Together." *Sociology Compass* 11, no. 5 (May 2017): e12466.

Nowakowski, Alexandra C. H., and J. E. Sumerau. "Reframing Health and Illness: A Collaborative Autoethnography on the Experience of Health and Illness Transformations in the Life Course." *Sociology of Health & Illness* 41, no. 4 (May 2019): 723–39.

Nowakowski, Alexandra C. H., and J. E. Sumerau. "Should We Talk about the Pain? Personalizing Sociology in the Medical Sociology Classroom." *Teaching Sociology* 43, no. 4 (October 2015): 290–300.

Nowakowski, Alexandra C. H., and J. E. Sumerau. "Swell Foundations: Fundamental Social Causes and Chronic Inflammation." *Sociological Spectrum* 35, no. 2 (2015): 161–78.

Omi, Michael, and Howard Winant. *Racial Formation in the United States*. 3rd ed. New York: Routledge, 2014.

Padavic, Irene, and Barbara Reskin. *Women and Men at Work*. Thousand Oaks, CA: Pine Forge Press, 2002.

Park, Kristin. "Choosing Childlessness: Weber's Typology of Action and Motives of the Voluntarily Childless." *Sociological Inquiry* 75, no. 3 (August 2005): 372–402.

Pascoe, C. J. *Dude, You're a Fag: Masculinity and Sexuality in High School*. Berkeley: University of California Press, 2007.

Pascoe, C. J. "Who Is a Real Man? The Gender of Trumpism." *Masculinity and Social Change* 6, no. 2 (June 2017): 119–41.

Pascoe, C. J., and Tristan Bridges. *Exploring Masculinities: Identity, Inequality, Continuity, and Change*. Cambridge: Oxford University Press, 2015.

Pascoe, C. J., and Sarah Diefendorf. "No Homo: Gendered Dimensions of Homophobic Epithets Online." *Sex Roles* 80 (February 2019): 123–36.

Pascoe, C. J., and Jocelyn Hollander. "Good Guys Don't Rape: Gender, Domination and Mobilizing Rape." *Gender & Society* 30, no. 1 (February 2016): 67–79.

Pfeffer, Carla A. "'I Don't Like Passing as a Straight Woman': Queer Negotiations of Identity and Social Group Membership." *American Journal of Sociology* 120, no. 1 (July 2014): 1–44.

Pfeffer, Carla A. *Queering Families: The Postmodern Partnerships of Cisgender Women and Transgender Men.* New York: Oxford, 2017.

Phillips, Scott, and Michael O. Maume. "Have Gun Will Shoot? Weapon Instrumentality, Intent, and the Violent Escalation of Conflict." *Homicide Studies* 11, no. 4 (November 2007): 272–94.

Pierce, Dignam, Douglas Schrock, Kristen Erichsen, and Benjamin Dowd-Arrow. "Valorizing Trump's Masculine Self: Constructing Political Allegiance during the 2016 Presidential Election." *Men and Masculinities* (2019). DOI: 10.1177/1097184X19873692.

Pirtle, Whitney N. Laster. "Racial Capitalism: A Fundamental Cause of Novel Coronavirus (COVID-19) Pandemic Inequities in the United States." *Health Education & Behavior* (2020). DOI: 10.1177/1090198120922942.

Pitt, Richard N. "'Killing the Messenger': Religious Black Gay Men's Neutralization of Anti-Gay Religious Messages." *Journal for the Scientific Study of Religion* 49, no. 1 (March 2010): 56–72.

Pitt, Richard N. "'Still Looking for My Jonathan': Gay Black Men's Management of Religious and Sexual Identity Conflicts." *Journal of Homosexuality* 57, no. 1 (2010): 39–53.

Ponticelli, Christy M. "Crafting Stories of Sexual Identity Reconstruction." *Social Psychology Quarterly* 62, no. 2 (June 1999): 157–72.

Prokos, Anastasia, and Irene Padavic. "An Examination of Competing Explanations for the Pay Gap among Scientists and Engineers." *Gender & Society* 19, no. 4 (August 2005): 523–43.

Prokos, Anastasia, and Irene Padavic. "'There Oughtta Be a Law against Bitches': Masculinity Lessons in Police Academy Training." *Gender, Work & Organization* 9, no. 4 (August 2002): 439–59.

RAINN (Rape, Abuse & Incest National Network). "About Sexual Assault." n.d. https://www.rainn.org/about-sexual-assault.

Rajunov, Micah, and Scott Duane (Eds.). *Nonbinary: Memoirs of Gender and Identity.* New York: Columbia University Press, 2019.

Raun, Tobias. *Out Online: Trans Self-Representation and Community Building on YouTube.* New York: Routledge, 2016.

Ravn, Signe. "'I Would Never Start a Fight but . . .': Young Masculinities, Perceptions of Violence, and Symbolic Boundary Work in Focus Groups." *Men and Masculinities* 21, no. 2 (June 2018): 291–309.

Ray, Rashawn. "'If Only He Didn't Wear the Hoodie . . .': Selective Perception and Stereotype Maintenance." In *Getting Real about Race: Hoodies, Mascots, Model Minorities, and Other Conversations*, edited by Stephanie M. McClure and Cherise A. Harris, 81–93. New York: Sage, 2015.

Ray, Rashawn, Melissa Brown, Ed Summers, and Neil Fraistat. "Ferguson and the Death of Michael Brown on Twitter: #BlackLivesMatter, #TCOT, and the Evolution of Collective Identities." *Ethnic and Racial Studies* 40, no. 11 (2017): 1797–813.

Rebchook, G., J. Keatley, R. Contreras, J. Perloff, L. F. Molano, C. J. Reback, K. Ducheny, T. Nemoto, R. Lin, J. Birnbaum, T. Woods, J. Xavier, and the SPNS Transgender Women of Color Study Group. "The Transgender Woman of Color Initiative: Implementing and Evaluating Innovative Interventions to Enhance Engagement and Retention in HIV Care." *American Journal of Public Health* 107, no. 2 (2017): 224–29.

Reese, Teri Jo. "Gendered Identity Work: Motivations for Joining the Military." Unpublished master's thesis, Florida State University, 2012.

Relman, Eliza. "The 25 Women Who Have Accused Trump of Sexual Misconduct." *Business Insider*, October 9, 2019. https://www.businessinsider.com/women-accused-trump-sexual-misconduct-list-2017-12.

Reskin, Barbara. "The Race Discrimination System." *Annual Review of Sociology* 38, no. 1 (2012): 17–35.

Rich, Adrienne. "Compulsory Heterosexuality and Lesbian Existence." *Signs* 5, no. 4 (Summer 1980): 631–60.

Richards, Tara N., and Kathryn A. Branch. "The Relationship between Social Support and Adolescent Dating Violence: A Comparison across Genders." *Journal of Interpersonal Violence* 27, no. 8 (May 2012): 1540–61.

Richards, Tara N., Kathryn A. Branch, and K. Ray. "The Impact of Parental and Peer Social Support on Dating Violence Perpetuation and Victimization among Female Adolescents: A Longitudinal Study." *Violence and Victims* 29, no. 2 (2014): 317–31.

Ridgeway, Cecelia L. *Framed by Gender: How Gender Inequality Persists in the Modern World.* New York: Oxford, 2011.

Robinson, Christine M., and Sue E. Spivey. "The Politics of Masculinity and the Ex-Gay Movement." *Gender & Society* 21, no. 5 (October 2007): 650–75.

Robinson, Christine M., and Sue E. Spivey. "Ungodly Genders: Deconstructing Ex-Gay Movement Discourses of 'Transgenderism' in the US." *Social Sciences* (2019). DOI: 10.3390/socsci8060191.

Robinson, Kristenne. "Violence against Women: Sociologists for Women in Society (SWS) Fact Sheet." Sociologists for Women in Society, 2009. https://socwomen.org/wp-content/uploads/2018/03/fact_05-2009-violence.pdf.

Rogers, Baker A. *Trans Men in the South: Becoming Men.* Lanham, MD: Lexington Books, 2020.

Rogers, James. "#MeToo: How an 11-Year-Old Movement Became a Social Media Phenomenon." *Fox News*, December 1, 2017. https://www.foxnews.com/tech/metoo-how-an-11-year-old-movement-became-a-social-media-phenomenon.

Rohlinger, Deana A. *Abortion Politics, Mass Media, and Social Movements in America.* New York: Cambridge University Press, 2015.

Roscigno, Vincent J., Lisette M. Garcia, and Donna Bobbitt-Zeher. "Social Closure and Processes of Race/Sex Employment Discrimination." *Annals of the American Academy of Political and Social Science* 609, no. 1 (January 2007): 16–48.

Rubin, Henry. *Self-Made Men: Identity and Embodiment among Transsexual Men.* Nashville, TN: Vanderbilt University Press, 2003.

Samuels, Ellen. *Fantasies of Identification: Disability, Gender, Race.* New York: New York University Press, 2014.

Sanders, Emile, Tamar Antin, Geoffrey Hunt, and Malisa Young. "Is Smoking Queer? Implications of California Tobacco Denormalization Strategies for Queer Current and Former Smokers." *Deviant Behavior* (2019). DOI: 10.1080/01639625.2019.1572095.

Scaptura, Maria N., and Kaitlin M. Boyle. "Masculinity Threat, 'Incel' Traits, and Violent Fantasies among Heterosexual Men in the United States." *Feminist Criminology* 15, no. 3 (December 2019): 278–98.

Scherrer, Kristin S., Emily Kazyak, and Rachel Schmitz. "Getting 'Bi' in the Family: Bisexual People's Disclosure Experiences." *Journal of Marriage and Family* 77, no. 3 (June 2015): 680–96.

Schilt, Kristen. "Just One of the Guys? How Transmen Make Gender Visible at Work." *Gender & Society* 20, no. 4 (August 2006): 465–90.

Schilt, Kristen, and Danya Lagos. "The Development of Transgender Studies in Sociology." *Annual Review of Sociology* 43 (July 2017): 425–43.

Schilt, Kristen, and Laurel Westbrook. "Bathroom Battlegrounds and Penis Panics." *Contexts* 14, no. 3: 26–31.

Schilt, Kristen, and Laurel Westbrook. "Doing Gender, Doing Heteronormativity: 'Gender Normals,' Transgender People, and the Social Maintenance of Heterosexuality." *Gender & Society* 23, no. 4 (August 2009): 440–64.

Schleimer, Julia P., Nicole Kravitz-Wirtz, Rocco Pallin, Amanda K. Charbonneau, Shani A. Buggs, and Garen J. Wintemute. "Firearm Ownership in California: A Latent Class Analysis." *Injury Prevention* (2019). DOI: 10.1136/injuryprev-2019-043412.

Schrock, Douglas. "Transsexuals' Narrative Construction of the 'True Self.'" *Social Psychology Quarterly* 59, no. 3 (September 1996): 176–92.

Schrock, Douglas, and Amanda Koontz Anthony. "Diversifying Feminist Ethnographers' Dilemmas and Solutions." *Journal of Contemporary Ethnography* 42, no. 4 (August 2013): 482–91.

Schrock, Douglas, Janice McCabe, and Christian Vaccaro. "Narrative Manhood Acts: Batterer Intervention Program Graduates' Tragic Relationships." *Symbolic Interaction* 41, no. 3 (August 2018): 384–410.

Schrock, Douglas P., and Irene Padavic. "Negotiating Hegemonic Masculinity in a Batterer Intervention Program." *Gender & Society* 21, no. 5 (October 2007): 625–49.

Schrock, Douglas, Lori Reid, and Emily M. Boyd. "Transsexuals' Embodiment of Womanhood." *Gender & Society* 19, no. 3 (June 2005): 317–35.

Schrock, Douglas, and Michael Schwalbe. "Men, Masculinity, and Manhood Acts." *Annual Review of Sociology* 35 (11 August 2009): 277–95.

Schrock, Douglas, J. E. Sumerau, and Koji Ueno. "Sexualities." In *Handbook of the Social Psychology of Inequality*, edited by Jae McLeod, Edward Lawler, and Michael Schwalbe, 627–54. New York: Springer, 2014.

Schwalbe, Michael, Sandra Godwin, Daphne Holden, Douglas Schrock, Shealy Thompson, and Michelle Wolkomir. "Generic Processes in the Reproduction of Inequality: An Interactionist Analysis." *Social Forces* 79, no. 2 (December 2000): 419–52.

Schwalbe, Michael, and Douglas Mason-Schrock. "Identity Work as Group Process." In *Advances in Group Processes*, vol. 13, edited by Barry Markovsky, Michael J. Lovaglia, and Robin Simon, 115–50. Bingley, UK: Emerald Group, 1996.

Schwalbe, Michael, and Michelle Wolkomir. "The Masculine Self as Problem and Resource in Interview Studies of Men." *Men and Masculinities* 4, no. 1 (2001): 90–103.

Scott, Marvin B., and Stanford M. Lyman, "Accounts." *American Sociological Review* 33, no. 1 (February 1968): 46–62.

Scully, Diana, and Joseph Marolla. "Convicted Rapists' Vocabulary of Motive: Excuses and Justifications." *Social Problems* 31, no. 5 (June 1984): 530–44.

Serano, Julia. *Whipping Girl: A Transsexual Woman on Sexism and the Scapegoating of Femininity*. Berkeley, CA: Seal Press, 2007.

Sewell, Abigail A. "The Racism-Race Reification Process: A Mesolevel Political Economic Framework for Understanding Racial Health Disparities." *Sociology of Race and Ethnicity* 2, no. 4 (2016): 402–32.

shuster, stef m. "Punctuating Accountability: How Discursive Aggression Regulates Transgender People." *Gender & Society* 31, no. 4 (August 2017): 481–502.

shuster, stef m. "Uncertain Expertise and the Limitations of Clinical Guidelines in Transgender Healthcare." *Journal of Health and Social Behavior* 57, no. 3 (September 2016): 319–32.

Silva, Eric O. "Public Accounts: Defending Contested Practices." *Symbolic Interaction* 30, no. 2 (Spring 2007): 245–65.

Simula, Brandy L., J. E. Sumerau, and Andrea Miller (Eds.). *Expanding the Rainbow: Exploring the Relationships of Bi+, Polyamorous, Kinky, Ace, Intersex, and Trans People*. Boston: Brill Sense, 2019.

Smith, Dorothy E. *The Everyday World as Problematic: A Feminist Sociology*. Boston: Northeastern University Press, 1987.

Smith, Jesse, and Ryan T. Cragun. "Mapping Religion's Other: A Review of the Study of Nonreligion and Secularity." *Journal for the Scientific Study of Religion* 58, no. 2 (June 2019): 319–35.

Snorton, C. Riley. *Black on Both Sides: A Racial History of Trans Identity*. Minneapolis: University of Minnesota Press, 2017.

Snow, David A., and Leon Anderson. "Identity Work among the Homeless: The Verbal Construction and Avowal of Personal Identities." *American Journal of Sociology* 92, no. 6 (May 1987): 1336–71.

Somerville, Siobhan. *Queering the Color Line: Race and the Invention of Homosexuality in American Culture*. Durham, NC: Duke University Press, 2000.

Spade, Dean. *Normal Life: Administrative Violence, Critical Trans Politics, and the Limits of Law*. New York: South End Press, 2011.

Steele, Sarah M., Megan Collier, and J. E. Sumerau. "Lesbian, Gay, and Bisexual Contact with Police in Chicago: Disparities across Sexuality, Race, and Socioeconomic Status." *Social Currents* 5, no. 4 (August 2018): 328–49.

Steele, Sarah M., Bethany G. Everett, and Tonda L. Hughes. "Influence of Perceived Femininity, Masculinity, Race/Ethnicity, and Socioeconomic Status on Intimate Partner Violence among Sexual-Minority Women." *Journal of Interpersonal Violence* 35, no. 1 (2017): 435–71.

Steffensmeier, Darrell, Hua Zhong, Jeff Ackerman, Jennifer Schwartz, and Suzanne Agha. "Gender Gap Trends for Violent Crimes, 1980 to 2003: A UCR-NCVS Comparison." *Feminist Criminology* 1, no. 1 (January 2006): 72–98.

Stewart, Evan, Jacqui Frost, and Penny Edgell. "Intersectionality and Power: Notes from the Editors." *Secularism and Nonreligion* 6, no. 6 (2017): 1–3.

Stone, Amy L. "Gender Panics about Transgender Children in Religious Right Discourse." *Journal of LGBT Youth* 15, no. 1 (2018): 1–15.

Stone, Sandy. "The Empire Strikes Back: A Posttranssexual Manifesto." In *Writing on the Body: Female Embodiment and Feminist Theory*, edited by Katie Conboy, Nadia Medina, and Sarah Stanbury, 337–59. New York: Columbia University Press, 1997.

Strauss, Anselm L. *Mirrors and Masks: The Search for Identity*. Glencoe, IL: Free Press, 1959.

Stryker, Susan. *Transgender History: The Roots of Today's Revolution*. New York: Seal Press, 2017.

Sumerau, J. E. *Cigarettes & Wine*. Boston: Sense Publishers, 2017.

Sumerau, J. E. "Embodying Nonexistence: Experiencing Mono- and Cisnormativities in Everyday Life." In *Body Battlegrounds: Transgressions, Tensions, and Transformations*, edited by Chris Bobel and Samantha Kwan, 177–88. Nashville, TN: Vanderbilt University Press, 2019.

Sumerau, J. E. "Experiencing Gender Variation." *Write Where It Hurts* (blog). December 16, 2015. http://writewhereithurts.net/2015/12/16/178-2/.

Sumerau, J. E. *Homecoming Queens*. Boston: Sense Publishers, 2017.

Sumerau, J. E. "I See Monsters: The Role of Rape in My Personal, Professional, and Political Life." In *Negotiating the Emotional Challenges of Conducting Deeply Personal Research in Health*, edited by Alexandra C. H. Nowakowski and J. E. Sumerau, 147–58. New York: Routledge, 2018.

Sumerau, J. E. *Palmetto Rose*. Boston: Sense Publishers, 2018.

Sumerau, J. E. "'Some of Us Are Good, God-Fearing Folks': Justifying Religious Participation in an LGBT Christian Church." *Journal of Contemporary Ethnography* 46, no. 1 (February 2017): 3–29.

Sumerau, J. E. "'Somewhere between Evangelical and Queer': Sexual-Religious Identity Work in a LGBT Christian Church." In *Selves, Symbols, and Sexualities: An Interactionist Anthology*, edited by Thomas S. Weinberg and Staci Newmahr, 123–34. Thousand Oaks, CA: Sage, 2013.

Sumerau, J. E. "'That's What a Man Is Supposed to Do': Compensatory Manhood Acts in an LGBT Christian Church." *Gender & Society* 26, no. 3 (June 2012): 461–87.

Sumerau, J. E., M. N. Barringer, and Ryan T. Cragun. "'I Don't Need a Shotgun, Just a Look': Representing Manhood in Secular and Religious Magazines." *Men and Masculinities* 18, no. 5 (December 2015): 581–604.

Sumerau, J. E., and Ryan T. Cragun. *Christianity and the Limits of Minority Acceptance in America: God Loves (Almost) Everyone*. Lanham, MD: Lexington Books, 2018.

Sumerau, J. E., and Ryan T. Cragun. "'I Think Some People Need Religion': The Social Construction of Nonreligious Moral Identities." *Sociology of Religion* 77, no. 4 (December 2016): 386–407.

Sumerau, J. E., Ryan T. Cragun, and Lain A. B. Mathers. "Contemporary Religion and the Cisgendering of Reality." *Social Currents* 3, no. 3 (September 2016): 293–311.

Sumerau, J. E., Ryan T. Cragun, and Lain A. B. Mathers. "'I Found God in the Glory Hole': The Moral Career of a Gay Christian." *Sociological Inquiry* 86, no. 4 (November 2016): 618–40.

Sumerau, J. E., Ryan T. Cragun, and Trina Smith. "'Men Never Cry': Teaching Mormon Manhood in the Church of Jesus Christ of Latter-Day Saints." *Sociological Focus* 50, no. 3 (2017): 213–27.

Sumerau, J. E., TehQuin D. Forbes, Eric Anthony Grollman, and Lain A. B. Mathers. "Constructing Allyship and the Persistence of Inequality." *Social Problems* (2020). DOI: 10.1093/socpro/spaa003.

Sumerau, J. E., and Eric Anthony Grollman. "Obscuring Oppression: Racism, Cissexism, and the Persistence of Social Inequality." *Sociology of Race and Ethnicity* 4, no. 3 (July 2018): 322–37.

Sumerau, J. E., and Lain A. B. Mathers. *America through Transgender Eyes.* Lanham, MD: Rowman & Littlefield, 2019.

Sumerau, J. E., Lain A. B. Mathers, and Ryan T. Cragun. "Incorporating Transgender Experience toward a More Inclusive Gender Lens in the Sociology of Religion." *Sociology of Religion* 79, no. 4 (Winter 2018): 425–48.

Sumerau, J. E., Lain A. B. Mathers, and Dawne Moon. "Foreclosing Fluidity at the Intersection of Gender and Sexual Normativities." *Symbolic Interaction* 43, no. 2 (2020): 205–34.

Sumerau, J. E., Irene Padavic, and Douglas P. Schrock. "'Little Girls Unwilling to Do What's Best for Them': Resurrecting Patriarchy in an LGBT Christian Church." *Journal of Contemporary Ethnography* 44, no. 3 (2015): 306–34.

Sweet, Paige L. "The Sociology of Gaslighting." *American Sociological Review* 84, no. 5 (2019): 851–75.

Taylor, Rae, and Jana L. Jasinski. "Femicide and the Feminist Perspective." *Homicide Studies* 15, no. 4 (November 2011): 341–62.

Thorne, Barrie. *Gender Play: Girls and Boys in School.* New Brunswick, NJ: Rutgers University Press, 1993.

Thumma, Scott. "Negotiating a Religious Identity: The Case of the Gay Evangelical." *Sociology of Religion* 52, no. 4 (December 1991): 333–47.

Time. "'Our Pain Is Never Prioritized': #MeToo Founder Tarana Burke Says We Must Listen to 'Untold' Stories of Minority Women." April 23, 2019. https://time.com/5574163/tarana-burke-metoo-time-100-summit/.

Tough Guise: Violence, Media, and the Crisis in Masculinity. Directed by Sut Jhally. Media Education Foundation, 2000.

Tough Guise 2: Violence, Manhood, and American Culture. Directed by Jeremy Earp. Media Education Foundation, 2013.

Trautner, Mary Nell. "Doing Gender, Doing Class: The Performance of Sexuality in Exotic Dance Clubs." *Gender & Society* 19, no. 6 (December 2005): 771–88.

Tudor, Andrew. "A (Macro) Sociology of Fear?" *The Sociological Review* 15, no. 2 (May 2003): 238–56.

Ueno, Koji, and Haley Gentile. "Moral Identity in Friendships between Gay, Lesbian, Bisexual Students and Straight Students in College." *Symbolic Interaction* 38, no. 1 (2015): 83–102.

Vaccaro, Christian Alexander. "Male Bodies in Manhood Acts: The Role of Body-Talk and Embodied Practice in Signifying Culturally Dominant Notions of Manhood." *Sociology Compass* 5, no. 1 (January 2011): 65–76.

Venema, Rachel M., Katherine Lorenz, and Nicole Sweda. "Unfounded, Cleared, or Cleared by Exceptional Means: Sexual Assault Case Outcomes from 1999 to 2014." *Journal of Interpersonal Violence* (2019). DOI: 10.1177/0886260519876718.

Vidal-Ortiz, Salvador. "The Figure of the Transwoman of Color through the Lens of 'Doing Gender.'" *Gender & Society* 23, no. 1 (February 2009): 99–103.

Vidal-Ortiz, Salvador. "Queering Sexuality and Doing Gender: Transgender Men's Identification with Gender and Sexuality." In *Gendered Sexualities (Advances in Gender Research, Volume 6)*, edited by Patricia Gagné and Richard Tewksbury, 181–233. New York: Elsevier Science Press, 2002.

Walters, Mikel L., Jieru Chen, and Matthew Breiding. *The National Intimate Partner and Sexual Violence Survey (NISVS): 2010 Findings on Victimization by Sexual Orientation.* Atlanta, GA: National Center for Injury Prevention and Control, Centers for Disease Control and Prevention, 2013. https://www.cdc.gov/violenceprevention/pdf/nisvs_sofindings.pdf.

Ward, Jane. *Not Gay: Sex between Straight White Men.* New York: New York University Press, 2015.

Warner, Michael. *The Trouble with Normal: Sex, Politics, and the Ethics of Queer Life.* Cambridge, MA: Harvard University Press, 1999.

Washington, Harriet A. *Medical Apartheid: The Dark History of Medical Experimentation on Black Americans from Colonial Times to Present.* New York: Harlem Moon, 2006.

Wesley, Saylesh. "Twin-Spirited Woman: Sts'iyóye smestíyexw slhá:li." *Transgender Studies Quarterly* 1, no. 3 (August 2014): 338–51.

West, Candace, and Sarah Fenstermaker. "Doing Difference." *Gender & Society* 9, no. 1 (February 1995): 8–37.

West, Candace, and Don H. Zimmerman. "Accounting for Doing Gender." *Gender & Society* 23, no. 1 (February 2009): 112–22.

West, Candace, and Don H. Zimmerman. "Doing Gender." *Gender & Society* 1, no. 2 (June 1987): 125–51.

Westbrook, Laurel, and Kristen Schilt. "Doing Gender, Determining Gender: Transgender People, Gender Panics, and the Maintenance of the Sex/Gender/Sexuality System." *Gender & Society* 28, no. 1 (February 2014): 32–57.

Wiest, Julie B. *Creating Cultural Monsters: Serial Murder in America.* Boca Raton, FL: CRC Press, 2011.

Wingfield, Adia Harvey. "The Modern Mammy and the Angry Black Man: African American Professionals' Experiences with Gendered Racism in the Workplace." *Race, Gender & Class* 14, no. 1–2 (2007): 196–212.

Wingfield, Adia Harvey. "Racializing the Glass Escalator: Reconsidering Men's Experiences with Women's Work." *Gender & Society* 23, no. 1 (February 2009): 5–26.

Wolkomir, Michelle. *Be Not Deceived: The Sacred and Sexual Struggles of Gay and Ex-Gay Christian Men.* New Brunswick, NJ: Rutgers University Press, 2006.

Worthen, Meredith G. F. "An Argument for Separate Analyses of Attitudes toward Lesbian, Gay, Bisexual Men, Bisexual Women, MtF, and FtM Transgender Individuals." *Sex Roles: A Journal of Research* 68, no. 11–12 (2013): 703–23.

zamantakis, alithia. "'I Try Not to Push It Too Far': Trans/Nonbinary Individuals Negotiating Race and Gender in Intimate Relationships." In *Expanding the Rainbow: Exploring the Relationships of Bi+, Trans, Polyamorous, Asexual, Kinky, and Intersex People*, edited by Brandy L. Simula, J. E. Sumerau, and Andrea Miller, 293–307. Leiden, The Netherlands: Brill Sense, 2019.

Zuckerman, Phil. "Atheism, Secularity, and Well-Being: How the Findings of Social Science Counter Negative Stereotypes and Assumptions." *Sociology Compass* 3, no. 6 (December 2009): 949–71.

Zuckerman, Phil. *Living the Secular Life: New Answers to Old Questions.* New York: Penguin Books, 2014.

Index

About the Author

J. E. Sumerau is an award-winning researcher, novelist, and professor of sociology as well as the director of applied sociology at the University of Tampa. Her research focuses on the intersections of sexualities, gender, health, and religion in relation to systemic patterns of violence and inequality. The author of more than 70 works to date, her work has appeared in countless academic journals, edited volumes, and as monographs from multiple academic presses. She is also the co-editor of the academic blog site www.writewhereithurts.net and a regular contributor to "Conditionally Accepted" at *Inside Higher Ed*. For more information on her work, please visit www.jsumerau.com or follow her on Twitter @JSumerau.